Computer Monitor Troubleshooting and Repair

Computer Monitor Troubleshooting and Repair

Written by:
Joseph Desposito
and
Kevin Garabedian

A Division of Howard W. Sams & Company
A Bell Atlantic Company
Indianapolis, IN

©1997 by Howard W. Sams & Company

PROMPT© Publications is an imprint of Howard W. Sams & Company, A Bell Atlantic Company, 2647 Waterfront Parkway, E. Dr., Indianapolis, IN 46214-2041.

International Standard Book Number: 0-7906-1100-7

Acquisitions Editor: Candace M. Hall
Editor: Loretta L. Leisure
Assistant Editors: Pat Brady, Natalie F. Harris
Typesetting: Loretta L. Leisure
Layout Design: Loretta L. Leisure
Cover Design: Suzanne Lincoln
Graphics Conversion: Christina Smith, Kelly Ternet, Phil Velikan, Christy Pierce
Illustrations and Other Materials: Courtesy of the Author, M I Technologies, Inc., Philips Consumer Electronics Company and Samtron

PRINTED IN THE UNITED STATES OF AMERICA

9 8 7 6 5 4 3 2 1

Table of Contents

X

Table of Contents vii

Chapter 1
Overview of Computer Monitor Circuits

A computer monitor is an output device for a personal computer. As such, its job is to accept electronic signals supplied by the computer, process the signals, and present them to the user in an intelligible way. When a computer monitor fails at its job, it is up to a technician to find out what is wrong and repair the problem.

Before a technician can attempt to repair a computer monitor, a good understanding of computer monitor circuitry is needed. This chapter serves as the starting point in gaining this knowledge by providing an overview of the major circuits.

1.1 High-Voltage Circuits

The high-voltage circuits are responsible for developing the high voltages needed for the anode and grids of the cathode ray tube (CRT). The anode of the CRT needs 20,000 to 30,000 volts depending on the size of the tube. This high voltage accelerates the electrons to a point where they can strike the phosphors at the front of the picture tube hard enough to produce light. This anode voltage is supplied by an integrated high-voltage transformer (IHVT) commonly called the flyback transformer.

Figure 1.1 shows a simplified block diagram of the high-voltage section of a computer monitor, including the CRT and flyback transformer.

The flyback transformer also produces the screen voltage, which goes to the second grid (G2) of the CRT and the focus voltage, which goes to the third grid (G3). The screen voltage is about 400 to 450 volts, while the focus voltage is about 5,000 volts.

The horizontal output transistor is considered part of the high-voltage circuits, since this transistor switches the flyback transformer. The horizontal output transistor is the most stressed part in the monitor.

High voltages are also developed in the power supply (which we will cover separately). The power supply supplies about 100 to 200 volts to the collector of the horizontal output transistor.

1.2 Horizontal Circuits

In order for the electron beam inside of the CRT to make a sensible picture, the beam has to be deflected from the point of ori-

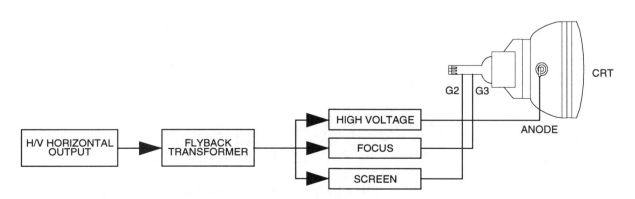

Figure 1.1. Simplified block diagram of the high-voltage section of a computer monitor, including the CRT and flyback transformer.

gin. In other words, the beam has to be deflected up and down, left and right. The horizontal circuits are responsible for deflecting the electron beam from left to right in a horizontal plane. A simplified block diagram of typical horizontal circuits is shown in **Figure 1.2**.

The horizontal circuits deflect the electron beam by energizing a coil around the neck of the CRT, called the horizontal deflection yoke. The horizontal lines traced on the screen of the CRT, for example 480 lines per frame in video graphics array (VGA) mode, combine to construct the picture you see on the computer monitor display. The horizontal deflection yoke is typically connected to the collector of the horizontal output transistor. This transistor produces the horizontal deflection pulses needed to deflect the electron beam.

The picture displayed on the CRT would be unintelligible if not for synchronization. For horizontal synchronization, the computer provides a horizontal sync signal. This signal synchronizes the horizontal oscillator in the computer monitor, which produces a signal for the horizontal drive transistor. The primary function of this

transistor is to drive the primary winding of the horizontal drive transformer. The secondary function of the horizontal drive transformer is to drive the horizontal output transistor, which drives the horizontal deflection yoke.

1.3 Vertical Circuits

The vertical circuits are responsible for deflecting the electron beam in the CRT up and down in a vertical plane. Without vertical deflection all you would see on the display is a horizontal line.

The computer sends a vertical sync signal to the monitor that varies in frequency depending on the current video mode. If the vertical frequency is 60 Hz, for example, the picture on the screen changes 60 times every second. This sync signal is sent to the vertical oscillator in the computer monitor.

The vertical oscillator produces a sawtooth shaped signal. This signal is amplified by a vertical output transistor. The amplified signal drives the vertical yoke. A simplified block diagram of the vertical circuits is shown in **Figure 1.3**.

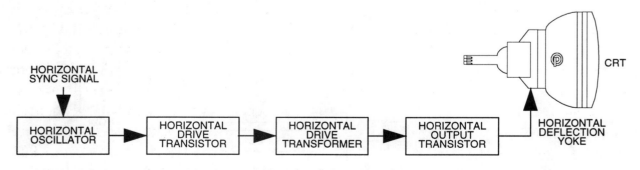

Figure 1.2. A simplified block diagram of typical horizontal circuits in a computer monitor.

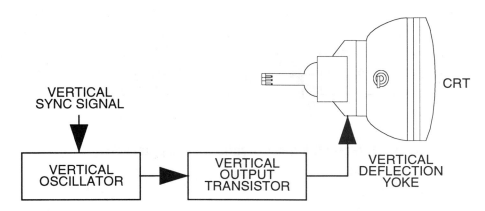

Figure 1.3. A simplified block diagram of the vertical circuits in a computer monitor.

1.4 Video Circuits

The video signals that come from the computer contain the information displayed on the computer monitor. In a color system, three video signals—red, green and blue—are sent from the computer to the monitor. The three video signals combine to make up the colorful pictures you see on the display.

Each video signal coming from the computer ranges from 0 to 0.7 volts. The job of the monitor's video circuits is to amplify these weak signals. This amplification, which is identical for each signal, is accomplished in several stages.

The final stage of amplification for each video signal is typically handled by a power transistor. Thus, there are three power transistors, one for the red video signal, one for the green, and one for the blue. Each transistor provides the current necessary to drive one cathode (red, green, blue) of the CRT. A simplified block diagram of the video circuits is shown in **Figure 1.4**.

1.5 The CRT

A cathode ray tube, or CRT, is a vacuum tube with a large rectangular face and a narrow cylindrical neck. This is the device responsible for displaying the information sent by the computer to the computer monitor.

Inside a color CRT are three cathodes—red, green and blue—which emit electrons when heated by a filament. There are also three grids. One accelerates the electrons, one focuses them, and one controls the brightness.

On the outside of the CRT, around the neck, are the horizontal and vertical yokes, which deflect the electron beams emitted by the three cathodes. Several magnet rings also surround the neck of the tube. These are used to converge the three beams, thus assuring color purity. At the back of the neck are the pins of the tube. These pins fit into a socket on the CRT printed circuit (PC) board. The anode (high-voltage) terminal is at the top center of the tube. A diagram of the CRT is shown in **Figure 1.5**.

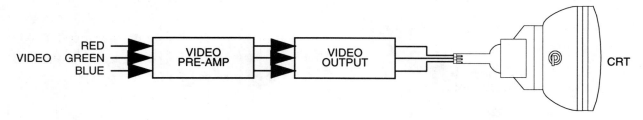

Figure 1.4. A simplified block diagram of the video circuits in a computer monitor.

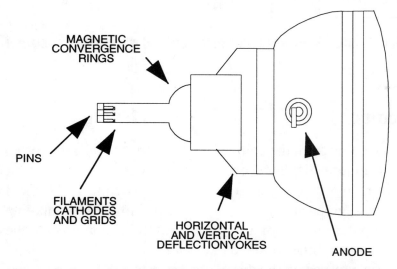

Figure 1.5. A simplified diagram of the CRT in a computer monitor.

1.6 Monitor Controls

Computer monitor controls vary the image that is displayed on the CRT. Some monitors have analog controls, some have digital, and some have both. Some controls are external, meant to be adjusted by the end user, and some are internal, meant to be adjusted only by a qualified technician.

The vertical controls, such as vertical size, position, center and linearity work in conjunction with vertical circuits. Horizontal controls such as horizontal sync, size, position, center, and linearity work in conjunction with the horizontal circuits.

The contrast and brightness controls are part of the video circuits, while the screen and focus controls are integrated into the flyback transformer. Other controls found on monitors are pincushion, trapezoid and parallelogram controls.

Analog controls usually use potentiometers. Varying the resistance of the potentiometer changes the voltage at a specific point in the control circuit. Digital controls, on the other hand, typically use pushbutton switches. Pressing the switch sends a signal to a microprocessor and then to a digital-to-analog (D/A) converter. The D/A converter produces a voltage, which varies the monitor control.

1.7 Microprocessor Circuits

Microprocessor circuits in a computer monitor typically include a microprocessor, a D/A converter and a memory chip. The main functions of the microprocessor are to process the signal coming from the digital controls of the monitor and to process the horizontal and vertical sync signals coming from the computer. The digital controls affect the image on the display. The vertical and horizontal sync signals provide the information needed for the monitor to automatically adjust itself to the current video mode of operation. Not all monitors have a microprocessor.

After processing the input signals, the microprocessor sends output signals to a D/A converter and also to other parts of the monitor, such as the power supply. The job of the D/A converter is to change the form of the signal from digital to analog. The resulting outputs are voltages, which are applied to various circuits of the computer monitor.

A memory chip is used to store the current settings of the monitor. This chip "remem-

bers" settings even when the monitor is turned off. When the monitor is turned on again, the stored settings are used to set up the monitor for operation. A simplified block diagram of the microprocessor circuits is shown in **Figure 1.6**.

1.8 Power Supply Circuits

As its name suggests, the role of the power supply is to provide power to the rest of the circuits in the computer monitor. The power cord of the power supply plugs into an alternating current (AC) outlet. In the United States, the AC line provides approximately 120 volts, alternating at a rate of 60 cycles per second (120 volts AC). The job of the power supply circuitry is to transform this 120 volts AC into the various AC and direct current (DC) voltages required by the other circuits in the monitor.

There are two basic types of power supply, linear and switch mode. In a linear supply, the AC line voltage is fed to the primary of a transformer. The secondary of the transformer produces the various voltages required by the monitor. Full-

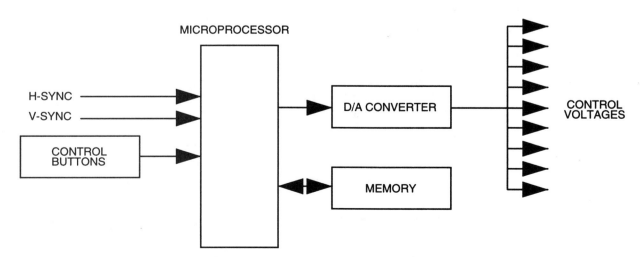

Figure 1.6. A simplified block diagram of the microprocessor circuits in a computer monitor.

wave (bridge) and half-wave rectifiers change the voltages from AC to DC. These "raw" DC voltages are fed to voltage regulators, which produce regulated DC voltages.

Linear supplies have been around longer than switch mode supplies. You'll find them in older monitors as well as in some newer models. **Figure 1.7** shows a simplified block diagram of a linear power supply.

The newer switch mode type of power supply works like a switch. Voltage from the AC line passes through a radio frequency (rf) filter, which is a small coil with capacitors connected to ground. The purpose of the filter is to suppress electromagnetic interference (EMI). The AC voltage is rectified by a bridge rectifier and filtered to produce a high DC voltage. A switching transistor converts this DC voltage back

to a square wave type AC voltage. The switching frequency of the transistor varies from about 50 to 100 kHz, depending on the load. This switching voltage is fed to a switch mode transformer.

Due to the switching action, the transformer takes current only part of the time. The secondary of the transformer produces the various voltages for the monitor. These are still AC voltages at this point. The AC voltages are rectified by special fast switching diodes to create DC voltages again and are then strictly regulated to produce the voltages required by the monitor.

The output voltage in a switch mode power supply is regulated through a feedback circuit. This feedback circuit typically includes an optoisolator that isolates the secondary side from the primary side of the power supply. A simplified diagram of a

Figure 1.7. A simplified block diagram of a linear power supply in a computer monitor.

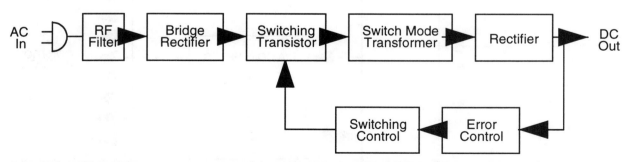

Figure 1.8. A simplified block diagram of a switch mode power supply in a computer monitor.

switch mode power supply is shown in **Figure 1.8**.

Keep in mind that the power supply always contains a fuse to disconnect power from the AC line if necessary. A blown fuse usually indicates further trouble in the power supply or in other circuits in the monitor.

Chapter 2
Tools and Test Equipment

To service computer monitors, you will need an assortment of tools and test equipment ranging from simple to sophisticated. Some monitor repairs can be completed with just a screwdriver, digital multimeter (DMM), and soldering iron. But, if you want to be ready to fix all the monitor problems that come your way, you will need to invest in some specialized gear. This chapter will give you a good idea of what's needed to do the job.

2.1 The Workbench

Before you begin to repair a computer monitor (or any electronic product for that matter), you need an area where you can perform the repairs. This area should have 3-prong (grounded) electrical outlets, good lighting, and a magnifying lamp. If you can afford it, you may want to invest in a workbench (see **Figure 2.1**). Some companies (Techni-Tool, Jensen Tools, etc.) sell special benches for electronic repair.

The workbench comes complete with a power strip and fluorescent lighting. Plus, there is a shelf where you can place your test equipment. This way, when you are working, your equipment is not staring you in the face. It doesn't clutter your work area. These workbenches cost several hundred dollars, but are worth the investment. Of course, if you are on a budget, you can do your repairs on a simple table.

If you don't own a workbench with built-in outlets, invest in good quality power strips with surge protectors. In your work area, you will need multiple outlets to hook up test equipment, monitors, soldering irons, magnifying lamps, and so forth.

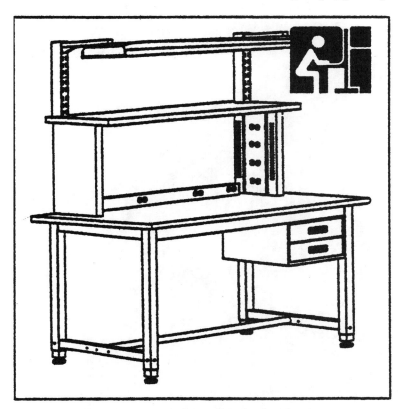

Figure 2.1. A workbench makes it much easier to accomplish your repair work.

Your work area needs a very good lighting system. It's very helpful to have a fluorescent light on the ceiling. You need to see what you are doing. Monitors have several printed circuit boards, all packed with electronic components. Without good lighting, you will have trouble identifying components. So, the better the light, the easier it is to work.

A magnifying lamp (see **Figure 2.2**) not only provides light, but also makes it easier to read component markings. When you repair a monitor, it is often necessary to check for cracks, broken solder joints, and burnt components. A magnifying lamp is perfect for this job.

2.2 Tools

You will need a good set of screwdrivers, with both Phillips and flat slotted heads. A power screwdriver is also a plus (see

Figure 2.3). Some monitors have so many screws that your hand will get tired unscrewing them. Not only do you need a Phillips screwdriver for removing the monitor's cabinet, but also to remove the extensive metal shielding used on some monitors. It is also advisable to have a Phillips-head screwdriver with a long (18" or more) shaft as shown in **Figure 2.4**. This tool is invaluable for getting at screws in tough-to-reach places. For example, you may need to unscrew a power transistor attached to a heat sink. These transistors are often hidden away at the far end of the monitor's circuit board under wire harnesses and are very tough to reach.

A long-nose pliers is needed to remove components once they are desoldered from the PC board (see **Figure 2.5**). Capacitors deep inside the printed circuit board are very difficult to remove without pliers. Wire cutters are useful for cutting wires

Figure 2.2. A magnifying lamp provides light, plus makes it easier to read component markings on the PC board.

Figure 2.3. A power screwdriver is a big help in disassembling a computer monitor.

Figure 2.4. A Phillips-head screwdriver with a long shaft can get at those hard-to-reach places.

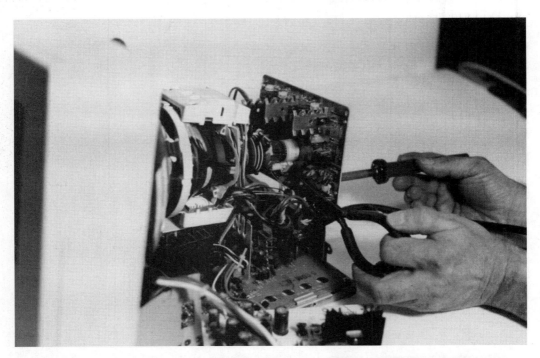

Figure 2.5. Long-nose pliers are needed to remove components once desoldered from the PC board.

and wire ties. Wire strippers are needed to cut away the insulation on a wire.

Probably the two most important tools needed for repair work are a good quality soldering iron and a desoldering tool. The soldering iron should be about 25 W to 35 W with an iron holder that sits on the workbench. The most popular desoldering tool is a hand action solder sucker. This tool is used together with a soldering iron (see **Figure 2.6**) to remove defective components, including integrated circuits (ICs), from the printed circuit board. Some desoldering tools work with a vacuum pump, but these are more expensive.

Solder braid is also useful for desoldering. This is a metal braid that you place over the solder you want to remove. You heat the braid with your soldering iron, and as the solder melts, the braid absorbs the solder.

You will need solder. For computer monitor work, purchase solder with .031" thickness. This allows you to solder in small areas. In other words, so you can perform the repair without spilling solder all over the place.

You'll need specialized tools, such as hex drivers. Sometimes, computer monitor manufacturers used hex screws to make it more difficult to service the equipment. Hex drivers will remove these screws. A set of nut drivers is a help, too. Some monitors, instead of using Phillips-head sheet metal screws, use screws with quarter-inch nut heads. So, you need a nut driver to open up the cabinet. Also, some components, such as power transistors, are mounted to heat sinks with quarter-inch metal screws secured with nuts. Sometimes, you can't get at the screw from the front and will need to loosen the nut from the back.

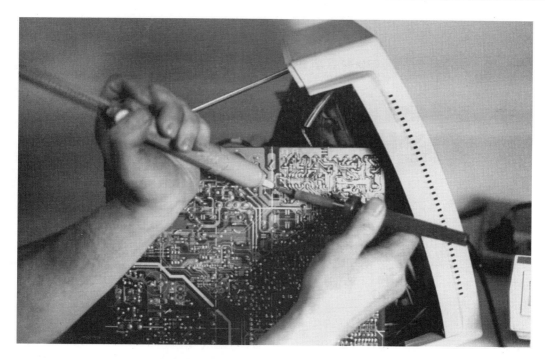

Figure 2.6. A desoldering tool is used together with a soldering iron to remove components from a PC board.

An IC puller is helpful for removing socketed ICs. You can also remove ICs with a small flathead screwdriver, but sometimes you can't position the screwdriver correctly. Also, it's easy to inadvertently bend the legs of an IC, if you don't remove it with the proper tool. An IC puller grabs the IC from the two ends and pulls it straight out of the socket without damaging anything.

A socketed light bulb is an important diagnostic tool, especially for power supply repairs or any repairs involving shorted components. Suppose you have found and replaced several shorted transistors. You may not be absolutely certain that you have found all the shorted components. If you don't want to destroy the parts you have just installed, it is a good idea to used a socketed light bulb in place of the monitor's fuse (simply clip the leads of the light bulb

to the fuse holder leads as shown in **Figure 2.7**). When you turn on the monitor, you will be able to tell if there are any more problems with the circuit—without destroying another fuse or some other components. If there are more damaged parts, the light bulb will shine brightly and stay that way. If the problem has been solved, the light will dim right away. The dimmer the light, the better.

2.3 General Test Equipment

In this section, we highlight general equipment for repairing computer monitors. Some equipment, such as a DMM, is an absolute necessity for the test bench. Other equipment, such as a transistor tester, is useful but not imperative to have. In any case, the more equipment you have, the more prepared you will be to troubleshoot all kinds of computer monitor problems.

Figure 2.7. A socketed light bulb can be used in place of the monitor's fuse when testing a repair.

Digital Multimeter (DMM)

An absolute must for servicing computer monitors is good quality DMM with a maximum DC voltage setting of at least 1,500 volts. A DMM is used primarily to measure voltage and resistance, but may also be used to measure current.

A high voltage setting is needed when you measure the voltage at the collector of the horizontal output transistor of a computer monitor. The collector will not only have a DC voltage, but also pulses of AC voltage. Normally, these transistors can withstand up to 1,500 volts of DC. When you make a measurement at this transistor, it's best to have a meter with a range of 1,500 volts. This way, the DMM doesn't get damaged, and you can comfortably measure the value of the DC voltage.

Most newer DMMs have a diode setting, marked with a diode symbol (see **Figure 2.8**). This setting is used for checking all of the solid state devices in the monitor, including ICs, diodes, transistors, SCRs, and so forth. If you have an older meter, you may not have the diode setting. If this is the case, you may want to consider purchasing a new DMM.

Your DMM should have good quality test leads. This is very important. Sometimes, in a monitor, you will be working in an area where there is 500 or 600 volts, especially at the screen pin of the picture tube socket. If the DMM leads are not high quality and do not have good isolation, you may get an electrical shock.

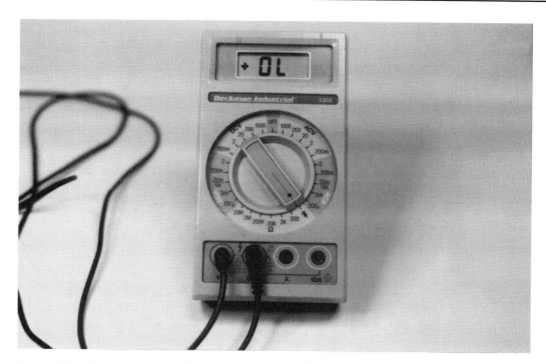

Figure 2.8. Many DMMs have a diode setting, marked with a diode symbol, for checking semiconductor devices.

Oscilloscope

An oscilloscope is a useful addition to the workbench. An analog scope with a 60 megahertz (MHz) bandwidth will serve you well. Most scopes work at 600 volts with test probes, but it is better to have a scope that works at 1,000 volts with test probes.

Don't get the idea that you'll need an oscilloscope for every repair. It is only needed every so often. For example, you may have a monitor repair where everything seems to be working, but there is no display on the screen. Without an oscilloscope, there is no way to trace the problem. A scope is also good when the vertical circuit is not working. With a scope, you can see if there is any signal going to the vertical output. The same holds true for the horizontal oscillator. You can check to see if the horizontal output is getting a signal.

Personal Computer (PC)

You may have never thought of a personal computer as "general test equipment," but a desktop or notebook PC is very helpful for servicing computer monitors. The graphics card in the computer, if it is a good quality card, will be capable of displaying most, if not all, of the current VGA, SVGA and higher video modes. You may not want to dedicate a computer to the repair bench; but, you should have one available to check certain video modes.

Transistor Tester

A transistor tester does a more thorough job of checking transistors than you can do with just a DMM. The transistor tester we use (see **Figure 2.9**) is the model 520B made by B&K Precision Instruments. This industrial type tester has three leads. You

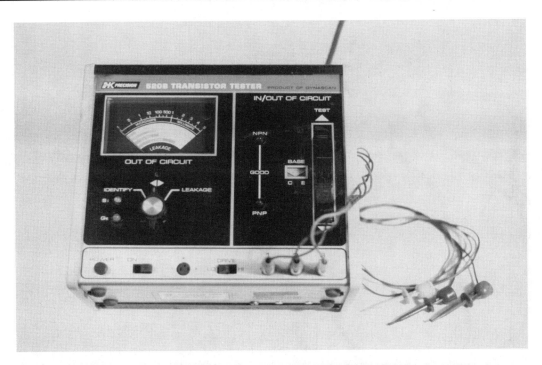

Figure 2.9. A transistor tester does a more thorough job of checking transistors than a DMM.

hook up these leads to the three leads of the transistor.

On the right side of the meter is a multiposition switch. You turn this knob until you get the right setting for the collector, base and emitter. At the left, a light comes on and tells you if the transistor is silicon or germanium. Another 2-position switch lets you know if the transistor is leaky. You turn the switch to the right and the meter indicates the extent of the leakage. This tester can also measure diodes.

A transistor tester is a very easy and fast way of checking transistors, but unfortunately this instrument is rather expensive, costing about $500.

Frequency Counter

A frequency counter is useful for checking the frequencies of, for example, the horizontal and vertical sync signals coming from the computer and the clock signal of the monitor's microprocessor. In our case, we do not have a separate instrument. Our frequency counter is integrated into our oscilloscope, a Sencore SC-61 (see **Figure 2.10**).

Power Supply

When you do computer monitor repairs, you sometimes need a bench-type power supply (see **Figure 2.11**) to test circuitry or to test components. We use a B&K Precision Instruments Model 1601, which is a regulated power supply. It has a voltage range from 0 to 50 volts on two ranges, 0 to 25 volts and 0 to 50 volts. Because of the limited range, you cannot supply power, for example, to the output circuits of a computer monitor. But the supply can be used with other circuits, such as video drivers, amplifiers and oscillators.

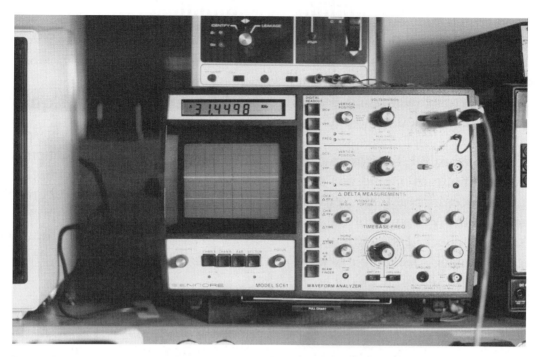

Figure 2.10. A frequency counter is integrated into the Sencore SC-61 oscilloscope.

Figure 2.11. A bench-type power supply is useful for troubleshooting computer monitors.

This supply has current limiting capabilities. This is a switch that you can set up to block current. This allows the power supply to cut off the power if you are afraid that the supply will damage some part. You can set the current to a lower rating. There are four ranges: 0.05, 0.2, 0.5 and 2 amps.

A power supply is useful, for example, if the monitor will not turn on and you suspect the microprocessor is at fault. You can place 5 volts on the Vcc input of the microprocessor and check if the outputs are producing any signals. An example of how the power supply is used to check the horizontal oscillator IC in a computer monitor is given in Chapter 9. You have to use a power supply wisely because sometimes the circuit is very complicated. Even though the circuit seems to be working when you supply power to it, associated circuits may be at fault.

There is a wide range of regulated bench supplies on the market. You should look for a supply with at least 15 volts and 2 amps voltage and current capability.

2.4 Specialized Test Equipment

In this section, we highlight specialized equipment for repairing computer monitors. As with an oscilloscope, this equipment is not necessary for every repair. But, as you will find out later, some repairs cannot even be attempted without certain kinds of equipment.

High-Voltage Probe

A high-voltage probe (see **Figure 2.12**) is the tool needed to measure the high voltage at the anode of the CRT. To make this measurement, connect the ground wire of the probe to the chassis of the computer monitor. Then, slip the probe tip underneath the suction cup of the anode clip.

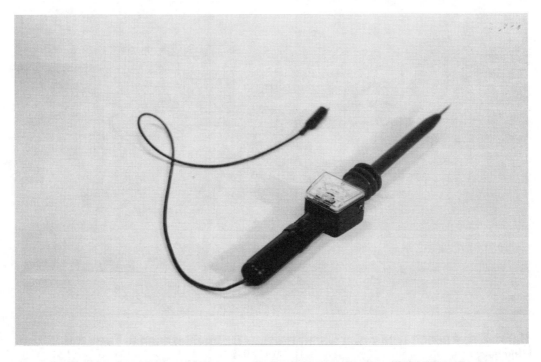

Figure 2.12. A high-voltage probe is the tool needed to measure the high voltage at the anode of the CRT.

Finally, touch the needle to the clip (see **Figure 2.13**). The voltage can be read on the face of the meter.

This measurement tells you if the high-voltage and horizontal sections of the monitor are working. It is also important because of the safety test you should perform on every monitor you repair. After the repair is done, and all adjustments have been made, you should check the level of the voltage going to the picture tube. Most monitors have a small sticker inside the case indicating the correct high-voltage level (see **Figure 2.14**). If this voltage level is exceeded, the radiation of the picture tube increases dramatically. This is a health concern.

People sit in front of the monitor for hours every day. If the high voltage is beyond the limit set by the manufacturer, then the picture tube is emitting heavy radiation. Picture tubes normally employ some kind of isolation, such as lead or some other material in the glass, which prevents the electrons from leaving the picture tube. But, higher voltages produce more power, and radiation may be able to get through the glass. And, of course, the person working at the computer monitor is the recipient of this radiation. So, for health reasons, it is important to check the high voltage at the picture tube with a high-voltage probe before you return it to the customer.

Computer Monitor Pattern Generator

A computer monitor pattern generator is a handy instrument for testing monitors. We use the Checker-12 from Computer and Monitor Maintenance (see **Figure 2.15**). It is a handheld portable unit. It is simple

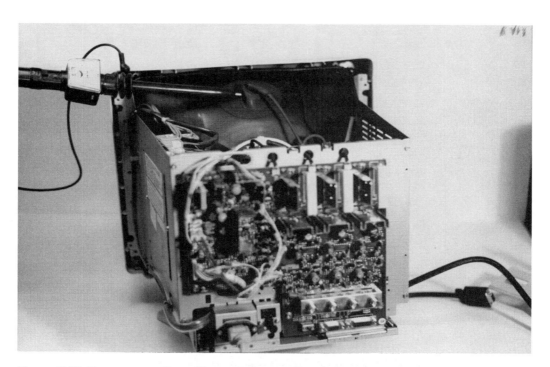

Figure 2.13. To measure the voltage at the anode, you have to touch the needle of the high-voltage probe to the clip of the anode wire. The meter shows the magnitude of the voltage.

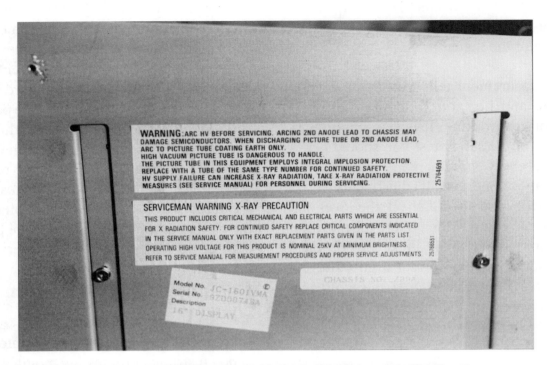

Figure 2.14. Most monitors have a small sticker inside the case indicating the correct level for the high-voltage.

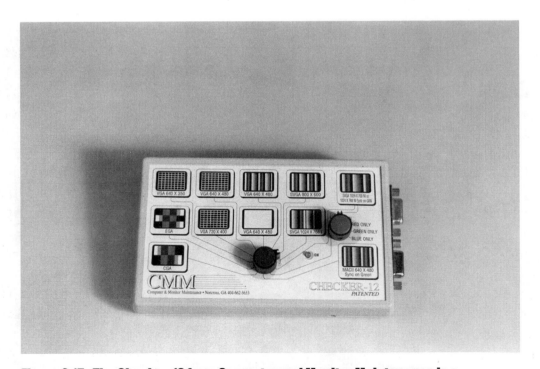

Figure 2.15. The Checker-12 from Computer and Monitor Maintenance is a portable pattern generator.

to use. Two rotary switches select mode, resolution, video pattern and video signal.

When a monitor comes into the shop, we connect it to the Checker-12 right away to find out what is wrong, rather than connecting it to a PC. If we need to, we can connect the monitor to a PC later on in the repair.

As a test instrument, a computer monitor pattern generator has an advantage over an IBM compatible personal computer. The Checker-12, for instance, can easily switch among VGA, SVGA, EGA and CGA video modes. With a PC, you are likely to have only VGA available. A PC (with a high-quality VGA graphics adapter) has an advantage over the pattern generator in that it can work in every VGA mode at all color levels. Other advantages of the Checker-12: it supports Macintosh II (640 x 480 sync on green) mode and 1,024 x 768 NI (non-interlaced) and NI sync on green modes.

The Checker-12 we use is an older model, which lacks certain Super VGA frequencies. So, it is not as useful as it could be for testing SVGA monitors. For example, we could not test 800 x 600 SVGA mode on a Magnavox Model 6CM320974I with the Checker-12. Although a quick glance at the Checker-12 may lead you to believe that it supports SVGA 800 x 600 mode, it does so only at a vertical sync frequency of 56 Hz. The Magnavox monitor, though, supports 800 x 600 mode with a vertical sync frequency of 60 Hz. If you try to display the Checker-12's 800 x 600 mode on this monitor, all you see is a distorted pattern. A newer model, the Checker-12E,

supports several more SVGA modes than the Checker-12.

The Checker-12 provides various test patterns for VGA monitors. The expected patterns are printed on the cover of the unit. The pattern and mode are selected with the single mode switch. A cross-hatch pattern is available in the three basic VGA modes. Color bars/gray scale and white screen are available in the 640 x 480 mode. This selection of patterns allows you to adjust all of the size and color balancing controls of a VGA or SVGA monitor.

The color bar/8-step gray scale (see **Figure 2.16**) assists in adjusting color balance and color tracking. The cross-hatch patterns assist in adjusting vertical controls (size, linearity and centering), horizontal controls (size, linearity and centering), and convergence.

A red switch controls the power and video output. You may select the complete video signal or one video output at a time (red, blue or green). The single outputs are useful for setting color purity and for single channel testing.

What does a computer pattern generator tell you? First, it tells you immediately if the monitor is capable of powering up and placing a pattern on its display. As soon as you turn on the generator, whichever pattern you select should appear on the screen. If not, you need to find out why. Next, the generator tells you whether the monitor is scanning correctly. If the monitor is overscanning, you will know right away from the look of the pattern. You will also know whether other monitor features are

Figure 2.16. The color bar/8-step gray scale pattern assists in adjusting color balance and color tracking on a computer monitor.

functioning properly such as contrast, brightness, pincushion, vertical and horizontal size, and vertical and horizontal position. If you are not familiar with these features, we will be covering them in detail later in the book. Finally, the generator tells you if all the colors are working (assuming the color bar pattern has been selected).

The Checker-12E is not the only device of its kind. CMM sells a whole line of these products. ICM (International Components Marketing) sells similar devices, including the MT802 Monitor Tester (see **Figure 2.17**). Computer pattern generators are available from other companies as well. If you decide to purchase this type of test instrument, review its features carefully.

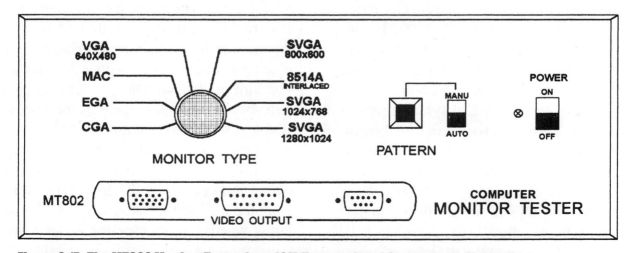

Figure 2.17. The MT802 Monitor Tester from ICM (International Components Marketing).

Make sure you understand all the modes and patterns it provides.

CRT Tester/Rejuvenator

As its name implies, a CRT tester/rejuvenator enables you to test and rejuvenate the cathode ray tube of a computer monitor. The one we use in our shop is a B&K Precision Model 467 (see **Figure 2.18**). We will go into some detail explaining how this device works, since we used it in one of our case studies.

The Model 467 can perform the following tests: leakage, emission, tracking, life expectancy, and focus electrode continuity. All tests are performed with power to the monitor off. Leakage tests indicate leakages between cathodes, or from any cathode to the heater, or to grid G1. The Model 467 has five leakage lamps. The lamps glow if the tester determines that leakage is occurring. For example, if the KB, KR,

and G1 lamps glow, it is an indication of leakage between the blue cathode, red cathode, and control grid.

Leakage between heater and cathode cannot be repaired, nor can excessive leakage between cathodes. Excessive leakage or a short between the control grid and cathode is a common fault in picture tubes. The tester can repair these common faults.

The emission test indicates the cathode emission current for each of the three electron guns. If the emission reads in the red (BAD) area, you can try to rejuvenate the tube with the rejuvenation feature of the instrument.

A 1.5 to 1 ratio limit exists for emission between the highest and lowest guns of the CRT. This feature is called tracking. If the tube does not track, you can use the cleaning and balancing feature of the tester to correct this fault.

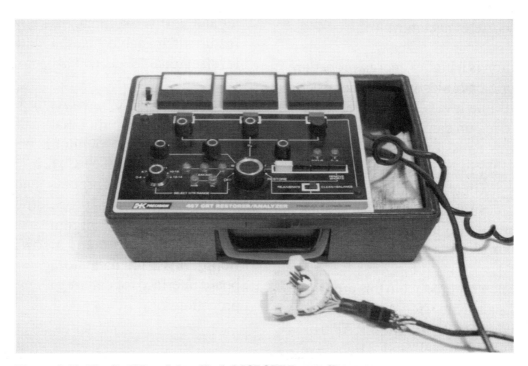

Figure 2.18. The B&K Precision Model 467 CRT Tester/Restorer.

The life test tells you whether the CRT will exhibit acceptable long-term performance. If the tester finds life expectancy to be poor, you can use the cleaning and balancing feature of the tester to correct this fault.

The focus electrode continuity test tells you if the continuity to the tube base pin is good. If the tube fails this test, the tester cannot correct the problem.

The Model 467 has three restoring functions: remove shorts, clean-balance, and rejuvenate. A low-resistance short (less than 20 kilohms) can be removed by the remove shorts procedure. High-resistance leakage is most successfully removed by the clean-balance procedure.

Cleaning and balancing is a low-energy restoring operation. It can be used safely on all tubes to eliminate surface contamination that causes high-resistance leakage or for further improving the emission of a fairly good cathode to restore tracking or to increase life expectancy.

Rejuvenation is a higher energy procedure for restoring cathodes when the emission is below usable levels. High-level rejuvenation of one gun can occasionally reduce the previous emission reading of another gun, particularly if that gun had just been rejuvenated. Therefore, after rejuvenation, it is often desirable to clean and balance one or more of the guns in order to achieve good tracking.

Sencore's newest product in this area is the CR7000 Beam-Rite CRT Analyzer & Restorer (see **Figure 2.19**). The CR7000 uses an exclusive "Lo Level" and "High Level"

emission track and detects all gun elements for shorts or leakage. The device also features six levels of "progressive" restoration for safe and effective restoration. The CR7000's sockets have a new design, which is meant to help you connect to hard-to-reach CRTs more easily.

Computer Monitor Analyzer

A computer monitor analyzer is an all-in-one piece of equipment designed especially to test computer monitors. Sencore's newest model is the CM2220 Computer Monitor Analyzer (see **Figure 2.20**). This instrument can completely troubleshoot, test and align high-bandwidth monitors. A special feature of the analyzer is its ability to perform color output analysis.

The CM2220 provides a complete and programmable RGB video generator with video bandwidth to 220 MHz, pixel resolution to 2,048 (horizontal and vertical), and scan frequencies to 250 kHz horizontal and 250 Hz vertical. The CM220 also features adjustable blanking times, color levels, signal levels and aspect ratio.

The exclusive integrated Auto "ColorPro" color analyzer is a tool that makes it easy to determine if the monitor is operating to factory standards. The CM2220 also features an interactive "process generator" for guided step-by-step processing through routine testing and alignments. This sophisticated instrument also features a floppy drive for data storage and a keyboard interface for entering alignments and procedures.

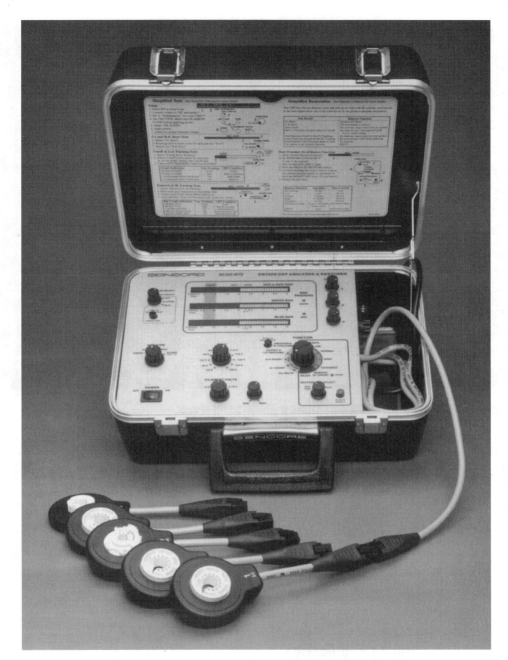

Figure 2.19. Sencore's CR7000 Beam-Rite CRT Analyzer & Restorer.

Monitor Test Software

If you prefer to use a personal computer rather than a dedicated computer monitor pattern generator for testing, you should invest in computer monitor test software. An excellent product in this area is *DisplayMate for Windows* from Sonera Technologies. *DisplayMate* is expert system software designed that shows end-users how to precisely set all of the parameters, controls and adjustments on both the computer monitor and the video adapter in the computer. The purpose of the program is to have the monitor and adapter

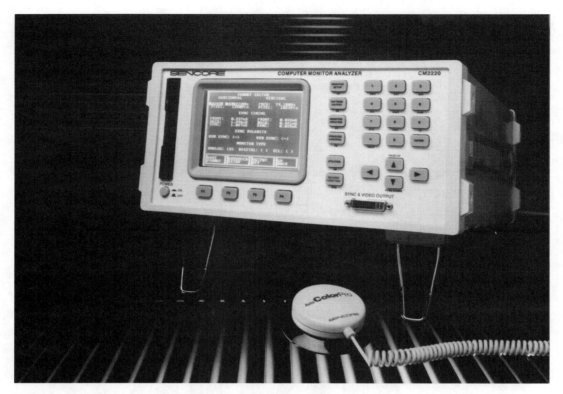

Figure 2.20. Sencore's CM2220 Computer Monitor Analyzer.

work together as an optimized system to produce the best possible image quality.

DisplayMate includes a *Set Up Program* and a *Tune-Up Program*. The *Set Up Program* shows how to quickly adjust the monitor to produce superior image quality. Then, the *Tune-Up Program* further improves and enhances the picture quality by systematically searching for every possible potential weakness of a computer monitor at very high sensitivity, and then showing how to improve the image at every step. Though designed for the end-user, this product is obviously a good one for technicians, too. A typical DisplayMate screen is shown in **Figure 2.21**.

A more general software product for testing computer monitors and all other parts of a computer system is *The Troubleshooter* from ForeFront. One of the nice features of this diagnostic software is its ability to self boot from a single floppy disk. This means you can use it with virtually any computer, old or new, desktop or portable. *The Troubleshooter*'s menu of video adapter tests is shown in **Figure 2.22**. To run a test, you simply select it from the menu.

Degaussing Coil

A monitor's built-in degausser is not as powerful as an external degaussing coil and may take a long time to demagnetize the picture tube. So, after you finish a repair, it is a good idea to demagnetize the picture tube before returning the monitor to the customer.

This procedure is done with a degaussing coil (see **Figure 2.23**). A degaussing coil is nothing but a large coil with a switch

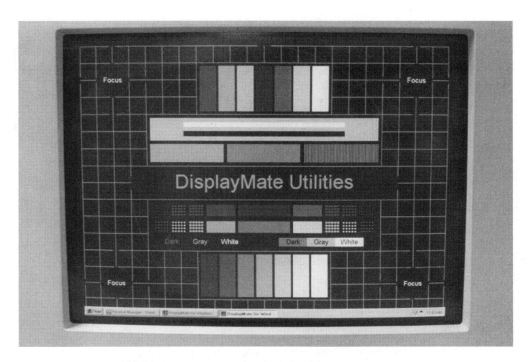

Figure 2.21. *DisplayMate's* master test pattern screen.

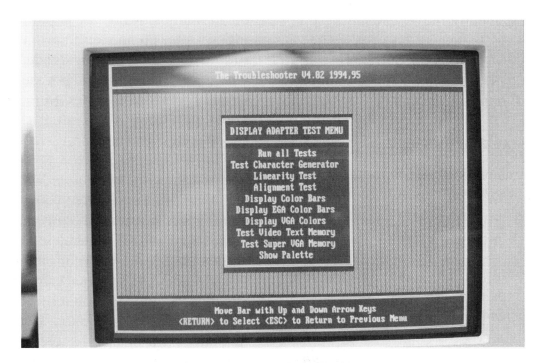

Figure 2.22. *The Troubleshooter's* menu of video adapter tests.

Figure 2.23. A degaussing coil can restore color purity to a computer monitor.

and a long power cord. The moment you turn the switch on, you must move the coil in a circular motion near the picture tube and then gradually move away from the tube. When you are seven or eight feet away, you can turn off the power. The picture tube will be demagnetized and the colors will return to normal.

2.5 Miscellaneous

There are many accessories that make computer monitor repair work easier to do. Jumper cables, power cords and chemicals are just a few, which we describe here.

Jumper cables are very handy. Sometimes during a repair, you have to bridge a capacitor or resistor that you suspect is defective. Jumper cables make it easy to do this. Or, you may want to make a solid connection to ground for your measurements. You can connect one end of a

jumper cable to the grounding point and the other end to the test probe. There are many kinds of jumper cables. Some have alligator clips, which are good for attaching to larger components such as capacitors. Some have spring-loaded hooks, which are good for tight spots such as the leads of transistors or ICs. Spring-loaded hooks help to avoid creating shorts between component leads.

You will need power cords, VGA cables and so forth. Sometimes, you will get a monitor in for repair which is missing its power cord and signal cables. The power cord is needed to power up the monitor, and a standard VGA signal cable is needed to supply a signal to monitor from a computer or a pattern generator. Many monitors have built-in signal cables, but some don't.

A more expensive type of signal cable is an RGB cable (see **Figure 2.24**). This is useful for testing monitors with RGB inputs (BNC connectors) in addition to the standard 15-pin VGA input connector. **Figure 2.25** shows a NEC Multisync 4D monitor attached to a signal source through its BNC input connectors. Note that a monitor with both BNC connectors and a standard 15-pin connector can be connected to two different computers, if desired. The NEC 4D has a switch on the front panel for switching between the two inputs.

Chemicals are often needed to complete a computer monitor repair. You will need lubricants, like a light oil, to lubricate variable (manual) controls. Contact cleaners are good for cleaning manual controls such as brightness.

You will need a freon-type chemical to help you track down temperature-related intermittent problems that occur in computer monitors. A product such as Freez-It from Chemtronics helps you locate the faulty component. You may notice that the computer monitor works well only after it warms up. If you suspect an IC, transistor or other component, you simply spray it. If the component you spray is the culprit, the problem will reoccur immediately (the spray lowers the temperature of the part).

Defluxers are needed to clean up areas that have been desoldered and soldered during the course of a repair. Defluxers help dissolve and remove flux residue. A small brush (a toothbrush is perfect) should be used in conjunction with the defluxer.

A heat gun does the opposite job of a freon-type spray. Some monitors work fine when you first turn them on and then exhibit problems after they warm up. A heat gun helps you diagnose the problem by giving you the ability to raise the temperature of a particular component or suspected area.

Components and controls inside of a monitor can accumulate a lot of dust. A can of compressed air is useful for blowing away the dust; a small vacuum cleaner is helpful for removing the dust.

There are many other accessories on the market that make it easier to do repairs. We have mentioned just a few of our favorites here. Most electronics parts catalogs include a complete range of repair accessories.

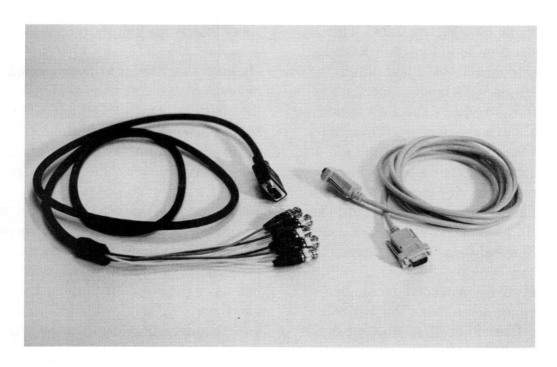

Figure 2.24. An RGB cable is useful for testing monitors with RGB inputs (BNC connectors).

Figure 2.25. An NEC Multisync 4D monitor attached to a signal source through its BNC input connectors.

Chapter 3
Monitor Types

The graphics system of IBM and compatible personal computers has changed radically since the introduction of the IBM PC back in 1981. The original PC used the monochrome display adapter (MDA), which connected to a digital monochrome monitor. Shortly after, IBM introduced the color graphics adapter (CGA), which connected to a digital CGA color monitor. The next advance in graphics technology for IBM and compatible computers was the enhanced graphic adapter (EGA), which connected to a digital EGA color monitor.

By this time, the computer industry was clamoring for faster speeds and more colors from their graphics adapters. IBM responded by introducing a radically different graphics system called the video graphics array (VGA). VGA adapters connected to *analog* VGA color or monochrome monitors. From this point on, the PC graphics system has been an analog system, with

further enhancements to resolution, speed, colors and so forth. For example, the 640 by 480 pixel VGA adapters were followed by the 800 by 600 super VGA adapters (SVGA). Monitors followed suit, sticking to the analog format.

3.1 Digital Monitors

Digital monitors, both color and monochrome, accept a digital video signal from the computer. These monitors are very much out of date and will not work with the current crop of personal computers.

How do you tell the difference between a digital monitor and an analog monitor? One of the tell-tale signs is a 9-pin connector at the back of the digital monitor (see **Figure 3.1**). All digital monitors that work with IBM and compatible computers have this connector. However, some older analog monitors use this connector, too.

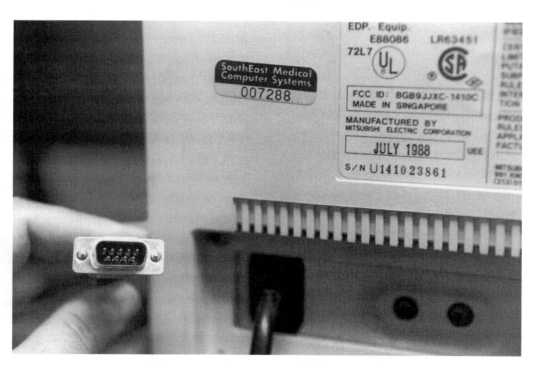

Figure 3.1. A tell-tale sign of a digital monitor is a 9-pin connector at the back.

If you get a monitor in for repair and it has a 9-pin connector, you'll need a computer monitor pattern generator to check it out. These instruments usually have provision for testing older monochrome, CGA and EGA monitors. You can quickly switch between modes to determine the type of monitor. If you do not have a pattern generator, you will need a PC with an older graphics adapter, one capable of providing a digital video signal to the monitor.

Since digital monitors are used with out-of-date PC graphics technology, we will not provide any details of their operation in this book. But, you still may be able to gain enough general knowledge from this book to repair a monitor of this type.

3.2 Analog Monitors

Analog monitors, both color and monochrome, accept an analog video signal from the computer. This is an important point. An analog monitor may have digital controls, for example, but this does not make it a digital monitor.

There are several different kinds of analog monitors that work with the current crop of IBM and compatible PCs. One type is the single frequency VGA monitor. Another type is the multiple frequency VGA/SVGA monitor. This type of monitor operates at two and sometimes three different frequencies. Still another type is the multiscan monitor, which works at all VGA and SVGA frequencies within its parameters. A multiscan monitor automatically reads the signal from the graphics adapter in the PC and compensates accordingly. The specifications of multiscan monitors include a range of vertical frequencies (e.g., 50 to 90 Hz) and a range of horizontal frequencies (e.g., 30 to 64 kHz).

All of these monitors have a standard 15-pin connector (see **Figure 3.2**) at the back or at the end of an integral signal cable. The signals at the pinouts of this connector are shown in **Figure 3.3**. One exception that comes to mind is the original NEC Multisync monitor (not the Multisync 4D referred to in this book, which is a later model). The original NEC Multisync monitor accepts both digital and analog video inputs and has a 9-pin connector. To connect this monitor to a VGA or SVGA graphics card, you must use a 9-pin-to-15-pin adapter.

All analog monitors with 15-pin connectors support the standard 640 by 480 VGA mode. Once you go beyond this standard mode, there is no guarantee that a particular monitor will work in a particular graphics mode. This is especially true of multiple frequency monitors. To test a multiple frequency monitor, you have to know the monitor's specifications, which are not always available. As mentioned in the preceding chapter, we tested a Magnavox Super VGA/60 (Model 6CM320974I) with the Checker-12. The monitor worked fine (after the repair) in standard VGA mode, but not in the Super VGA mode of the Checker-12. This was not the fault of the monitor or the tester! The two pieces of equipment were working in different SVGA modes. To test the Magnavox monitor in SVGA mode, we needed to connect it to a personal computer, which could display the correct mode.

Another problem crops up with multiple frequency monitors. Graphics cards and

Figure 3.2. A standard PC 15-pin connector (left) and a 15-pin Macintosh connector (right).

15 PIN "D"-SHELL CONNECTOR

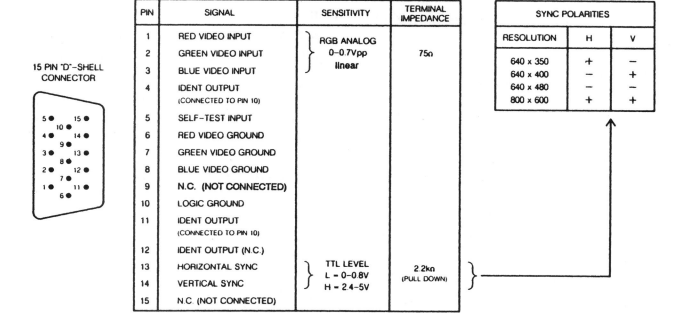

PIN	SIGNAL	SENSITIVITY	TERMINAL IMPEDANCE
1	RED VIDEO INPUT	RGB ANALOG	
2	GREEN VIDEO INPUT	0–0.7Vpp	75Ω
3	BLUE VIDEO INPUT	linear	
4	IDENT OUTPUT (CONNECTED TO PIN 10)		
5	SELF–TEST INPUT		
6	RED VIDEO GROUND		
7	GREEN VIDEO GROUND		
8	BLUE VIDEO GROUND		
9	N.C. (NOT CONNECTED)		
10	LOGIC GROUND		
11	IDENT OUTPUT (CONNECTED TO PIN 10)		
12	IDENT OUTPUT (N.C.)		
13	HORIZONTAL SYNC	TTL LEVEL	2.2kΩ
14	VERTICAL SYNC	L = 0–0.8V	(PULL DOWN)
15	N.C. (NOT CONNECTED)	H = 2.4–5V	

SYNC POLARITIES		
RESOLUTION	H	V
640 x 350	+	−
640 x 400	−	+
640 x 480	−	−
800 x 600	+	+

Figure 3.3. The signals at the pinouts of the standard PC 15-pin connector.

monitors are supposed to follow the same video standards as outlined by Video Electronics Standards Association (VESA). Sometimes, one or the other slightly varies from the standard. When this happens, you cannot get a display on the monitor. This type of incompatibility can lead to the conclusion that the monitor is somehow defective. Usually, all that is needed to make the graphics adapter and monitor compatible is a slight adjustment of the horizontal hold or vertical hold control. This is rarely an end-user control. In most cases, to make this slight adjustment, you must remove the monitor's cabinet and track down the appropriate control.

Although you rarely see them anymore, monochrome analog VGA monitors do exist. Standard VGA/SVGA color adapters work fine with monochrome monitors. Pattern generators work with these monitors, too, displaying a gray-scale pattern instead of color bars. Monochrome monitors use the green video input and ignore the red and blue video inputs on the 15-pin connector.

Throughout this book, we will highlight three analog monitors: the Magnavox 6CM320974I, a 14" multiple frequency SVGA color monitor with analog controls; the NEC Multisync 4D, a 16" multiscanning color monitor with digital controls; and the Samtron SC-728SXL, a 17" multiscanning color monitor with digital controls and an on-screen display.

Before we leave this section, we must mention that certain analog monitors do not adhere to the VGA standard. Years ago, when Apple II+ computers (and others of

that type) were popular, you could connect them to analog monitors. These monitors, which have composite video inputs (RCA jacks), are still used today for video games, VCRs, and other equipment with a composite video output (see **Figure 3.4**). Although we will not offer details of operation for this type of analog monitor, you still may be able to gain enough general knowledge from this book to repair a monitor of this type.

3.3 Multimedia Monitors

Many computer systems include so-called multimedia monitors. These monitors are standard analog type multifrequency or multiscanning monitors with a built-in microphone and speaker volume control. Speakers are either attached to the side of the monitor or integrated into the monitor's cabinet. At the rear of the monitor are the speaker and microphone outputs.

There is no complex sound circuitry in a multimedia monitor. The PC sound circuits are typically on a sound card or on the motherboard inside the system unit of a personal computer. Thus, when repairing a multimedia monitor, you will not have to spend time troubleshooting mono or stereo sound circuitry.

3.4 Computer Video Modes

It would certainly be easier to troubleshoot and repair computer monitors if all of them followed the same cookie-cutter design. As is evident from this chapter, this is not nearly the case. In this section, we provide information on the popular video modes produced by a typical graphics adapter.

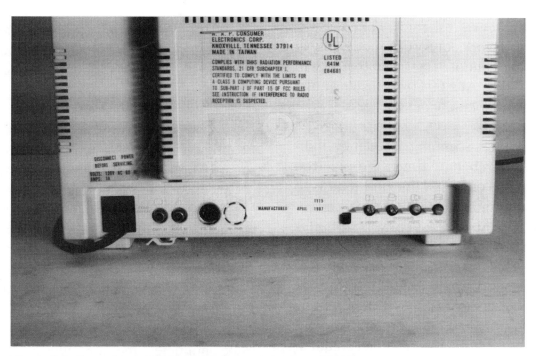

Figure 3.4. A monitor with RCA jacks for composite video input.

When you install a graphics adapter in a PC compatible personal computer running under Microsoft Windows, you get to choose the resolution and number of colors you want to display on your computer monitor. Limits to resolution and color depend on the capability of the graphics adapter. In general, the higher the resolution and the more the colors you desire, the more memory you will need on the graphics adapter. Typically, you will choose one of the following resolutions: VGA (640 x 480); SVGA (800 x 600); 1,024 x 768; or 1,280, x 1,024. The number of colors generally available is: 16; 256; 32K; 65K; or 16.8M. For each combination of resolution and color, the graphics card will output a specific vertical and horizontal frequency based on video standards set forth by VESA. These signals are sent to the monitor. Appendix B lists current VESA and other video standards.

The vertical scanning frequency indicates the number of times the electron beam of the CRT sweeps the entire screen and returns to the beginning of the next screen in one second. A scanning frequency of 72 Hz means the screen is completely scanned 72 times per second. The vertical scanning frequency is different for each resolution (640 x 480, 800 x 600, etc.), and also can differ within a specific resolution (e.g. 800 x 600). Multiscan monitors automatically recognize the vertical scanning frequency and compensate for the timing differences.

The vertical scanning frequency is sometimes referred to as the refresh rate. At certain refresh rates the user may notice flicker on the screen. The ability to detect flicker varies from person to person. In general, a flicker-free refresh rate is considered to be 70 Hz or higher. If a person complains about flicker, there is no way to solve the problem unless the monitor can work at higher refresh rates. For example, if a monitor works in SVGA mode only at 60 Hz, you cannot "fix" it so that it will work at 72 Hz. At a 60 Hz refresh rate, the user may complain about flicker.

The horizontal scanning frequency indicates the number of times the electron beam sweeps one scan line and returns to the beginning of the next line in one second. A scanning frequency of 64 kHz means 64,000 lines are scanned per second. Multiscan monitors automatically recognize the horizontal scanning frequency and compensate for timing differences.

If you want to find out the exact frequencies the graphics adapter is sending to the monitor, connect a frequency counter to the adapter (see **Figure 3.5** and **Figure 3.6**).

Select a good ground for the counter and then check the horizontal sync frequency at pin 13 and vertical sync frequency at pin 14.

One last point before we leave this chapter. The video modes in use today are primarily non-interlaced modes. In a non-interlaced system each frame contains all the scan lines (information) required to display a picture. In an interlaced system, a frame contains only one-half the number of scan lines required to display a picture. After each line is scanned, a space equal to the width of a scan line is skipped. The next frame fills in the skipped lines. The eye does not detect the missing scan lines due to the persistence of the phosphor on the CRT screen.

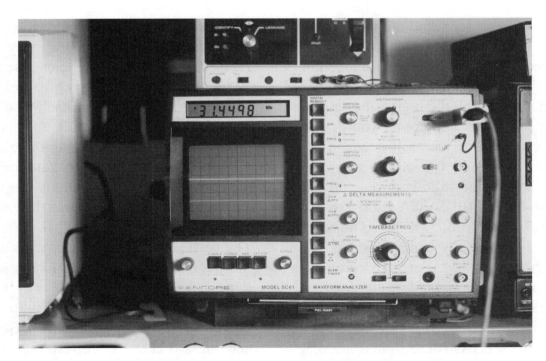

Figure 3.5. A frequency counter will tell you the frequency of the horizontal sync signal at pin 13 of the 15-pin connector.

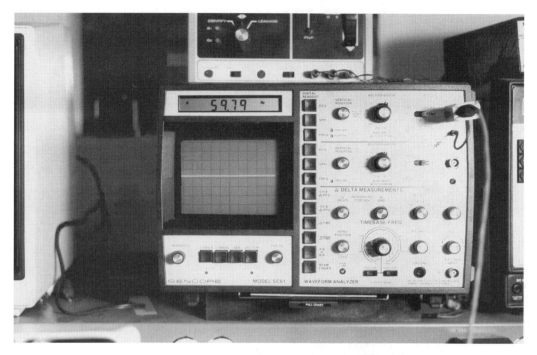

Figure 3.6. A frequency counter will tell you the frequency of the vertical sync signal at pin 14 of the 15-pin connector.

Chapter 4
Safety Procedures

Every time you open up a computer monitor for repair, keep in mind that voltages may be present in the set—even if the monitor is unplugged from the electricity. The CRT, for example, can hold a voltage for days, even though the monitor has not been used. This is not the only potential danger. In this section we explain how to protect yourself from dangerous electrical shocks when servicing computer monitors.

4.1 Grounding the CRT Anode

The CRT holds a charge long after the monitor is turned off, because it acts like a very large capacitor. The CRT actually has a capacitance, which is used for filtering the high voltage coming from the flyback transformer. The value of the capacitance is about 100 to 150 picofarads (pF). The dielectric is air and the electrical series resistance is very low. Thus, the high voltage remains for many days. So, when you service a computer monitor, keep in mind that electricity is there at the anode of the CRT.

In order to work safely on a monitor, you should discharge this voltage. How is this done? It's done with a long metal screwdriver and a jumper cable (see **Figure 4.1**). Clip one end of the jumper cable to the chassis of the CRT, which is an excellent grounding point, and clip the other side of the cable to the metal shaft of the screwdriver. Hold the screwdriver by its plastic handle with one hand and place your other hand behind your back. Place the metal shaft of the screwdriver under the rubber cover of the anode cap and touch shaft to the anode wire. To make sure there is no electricity left, you have to discharge the anode a few times, since each time you discharge it there is still a small voltage

Figure 4.1. Discharging the voltage at the anode of the CRT with a long metal screwdriver and a jumper cable connected to ground.

left. Once the CRT is discharged, it is safe to work on the monitor. If you need to, you can remove the anode cap without fear of electrical shock. Removing the anode cap is necessary when you change the flyback transformer, check the anode cable, and so forth.

4.2 Discharging Power Supply Capacitors

Another place in the monitor that holds electricity is the large capacitor in the power supply used for filtering the B+ voltage. This capacitor holds about 150 to 160 volts, which comes from the AC power line, and is rectified and filtered. If you are going to work on the power supply circuits, it's a good idea to discharge that capacitor. If the capacitor is not too large, you can easily discharge it with a small screwdriver. While holding the plastic handle, simply place the screwdriver's shaft between the plus and the minus leads of the capacitor (see **Figure 4.2**).

Sometimes this capacitor is higher in value, say 500 microfarads (μF). It holds a heavier charge of electricity. It may melt the copper on the printed circuit board or the tip of the screwdriver when you try to discharge it. A very good way of discharging a larger value capacitor is to place the leads of a socketed 100 watt electric light on the leads of the capacitor (see **Figure 4.3**). The capacitor is discharged very safely through the resistance of the lightbulb without any sparks and without burning or otherwise damaging the printed circuit board. One more thing, make sure the alligator clips on the leads of the socketed bulb are insulated with rubber covers.

4.3 More Grounding Considerations

When you use a DMM or any other meter to measure the voltages in the horizontal section or in the power supply, keep in mind that some of the monitors have a so-called split ground. One is a hot ground and one is a cold ground. This is especially true for monitors with a switch mode power supply (which most VGA/SVGA monitors have). **Figure 4.4** shows the location of the hot ground in the switch mode power supply of the Magnavox 6CM 320974I monitor.

When you ground your meter, pay attention to the circuit you are measuring. For example, if you are measuring the horizontal circuit, you must use the horizontal circuit ground for that purpose. It is very easy to find out where this ground is. Normally, it is connected to the emitter of the horizontal output transistor. If you use this point, it is a sure bet that you are using the right ground. If you use the ground of the power supply, you may destroy the meter, destroy the circuitry, or get a wrong reading, since you are using the wrong ground point.

Also, a danger exists if you try to use AC-powered test equipment, such as an oscilloscope, to make measurements on a computer monitor. In a monitor with a switch mode power supply (transformerless chassis) both the hot ground and cold ground are connected to the electrical line. If you attach the oscilloscope's ground wire to the wrong ground in the monitor and make a measurement, you can create a short. This will destroy transistors, diodes, ICs and other components in the monitor and will

Figure 4.2. Discharging a small electrolytic capacitor by shorting the leads with a screwdriver.

Figure 4.3. Discharging a large electrolytic capacitor by connecting a socketed light bulb to its leads.

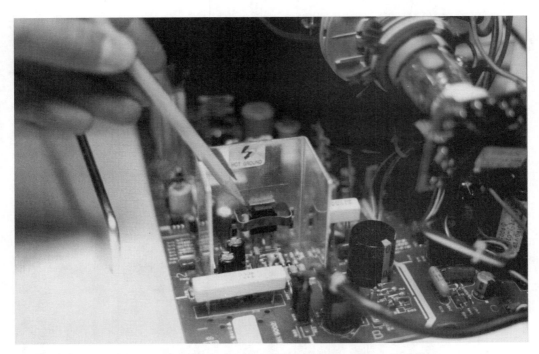

Figure 4.4. The hot ground in the switch mode power supply of the Magnavox 6CM320974I monitor.

melt the common lead or scope probe, too. You can avoid this situation by using an isolation transformer.

An isolation transformer is a transformer with a primary and secondary that is essentially the same (there is no step-up or step-down of the voltage). The primary is not directly connected to the secondary so it provides isolation from the electrical ground. To use an isolation transformer, you simply plug it into the AC line. The monitor and test equipment are then plugged into the outlets on the isolation transformer. With this setup you will protect yourself from an electrical shock.

If you are wondering where to buy an isolation transformer, look no further than your test equipment catalog. Any outfit that sells test equipment, such as Techni-Tool, also carries isolation transformers.

Chapter 5

Making Measurements

The most important part of the repair process is making measurements of voltage, current and resistance. The results tell you what is wrong with the computer monitor—if you have made the measurements correctly. In this chapter, we cover the techniques you need to know to make proper voltage, current and resistance measurements with a DMM.

5.1 Making Voltage and Current Measurements

Voltages are measured in parallel with the circuit you are checking. That is, you place the positive lead of the DMM at the point to be measured and the negative lead at a ground point. Most voltage measurements are made from the foil side of the printed circuit board rather than the component side (see **Figure 5.1**).

Current, on the other hand, is measured in series. In other words, in order to measure the current you have to disconnect some component from the circuit. Instead of that component, you place the DMM in series in the circuit where you want to measure the current. To measure voltages, you don't have to disconnect anything.

For the most part, you will *not* be making current measurements. Most of the measurements you make will be voltage and resistance measurements. If you have the schematic diagram of the monitor, you can make comparative measurements very easily. For example, you can check a particular pin of an IC or the collector, base, or emitter of a transistor to find out if the voltages at these points are correct.

Figure 5.1. Most voltage measurements are made from the foil side of the printed circuit board rather than the component side.

When you have a dead monitor, it's important to check the voltages at the power supply. Start the measurement by touching or connecting the negative lead of the DMM to ground. It's very easy to find the ground. Normally, the ground goes to the negative (-) lead of a large capacitor (this capacitor filters the DC voltage coming from the rectifier diodes). The negative lead of the capacitor is clearly marked on the can. Look for the copper trace on the printed circuit board that connects to the minus lead of the capacitor. This is the ground trace. You place the black (negative) lead of the DMM at this ground point and measure voltage with the red (positive) lead. You can move the red lead of the DMM around from point to point, while leaving the black lead clipped or hooked to the ground point.

5.2 Resistance Measurements

Resistance measurements can be made in-circuit and out-of-circuit. In-circuit resistance measurements should be made only after the monitor is disconnected from the power. Also, the power filters—the capacitors—must be discharged properly. Otherwise, you may destroy your DMM. Once the capacitors are discharged, you may begin measuring resistance.

Resistance measurements are made in parallel with the component you are measuring. In other words, you place the DMM leads across the leads of the component (see **Figure 5.2**). Like voltage measurements, resistance measurements are most easily made on the foil side of the printed circuit board. When you measure a resistance in-circuit, you may not be measur-

Figure 5.2. To measure resistance, place the DMM leads across the leads of the resistor.

ing the actual resistance of the component. If you really want the actual resistance, you have to disconnect one lead of the component from the circuit and then measure the resistance. Let's say you measure the resistance of a voltage regulator in-circuit. If you get suspicious that the resistance is very low, then you should disconnect the leads of the regulator and measure it out of the circuit.

Resistance measurements, as you can see, are not meant only for resistors. You can check the resistance of diodes, transistors and ICs, too. In fact, measuring the resistance of solid state devices such as those just mentioned is an excellent way of checking if there are any shorts in the circuit. For example, measuring resistance between two pins of an integrated circuit tells little except whether the IC has a dead short or not. This is all you can measure

because ICs are complex devices containing resistors and transistors. Basically, you are looking for a short (zero or very low resistance); you are not looking to measure the resistance. Whenever you make resistance measurements on solid state devices, the DMM should be placed in the diode resistance measurement mode (see **Figure 5.3**).

Diodes are fairly easy to check with a DMM set to the diode mode. Depending on the power of the diode, one measurement should be about 500 ohms. This measurement is made with the negative lead of the DMM on the cathode of the diode and the positive lead of the DMM on the anode (see **Figure 5.4a**). The other measurement should show an infinite resistance. This measurement is the reverse of the previous one (see **Figure 5.4b**). Note that some very powerful diodes measure

Figure 5.3. Whenever you make resistance measurements on solid-state devices, the DMM should be placed in the diode resistance measurement mode.

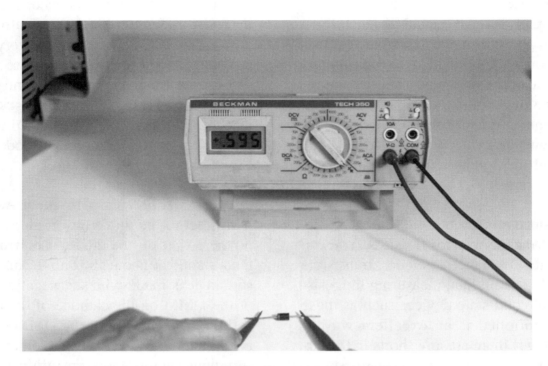

Figure 5.4a. A typical diode measurement in the forward direction.

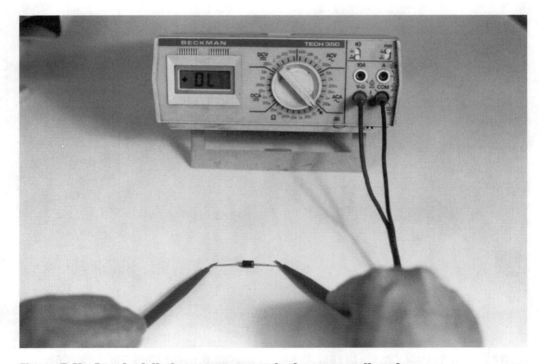

Figure 5.4b. A typical diode measurement in the reverse direction.

less that 500 ohms, about 450 to 470 ohms. In general, diodes are easy to check. Most of the time, you can make the measurement in-circuit. However, if there are any components in parallel with the diode, you should disconnect one side of the diode from the circuit before making the measurement. A bad diode may be shorted (low resistance in both directions) or open (infinite resistance in both directions).

Transistors can be checked with the DMM set to the diode setting. You can make the measurement either in-circuit or out-of-circuit. If you get a reading that is not acceptable, then you should desolder the transistor from the printed circuit board and take it out of the circuit. Then, you can measure it either with a DMM in the diode mode or with a transistor tester such as the one described in Chapter 2.

With the DMM, you measure the resistance between the base and the collector and between the base and emitter of the transistor (see **Figure 5.5**). You cannot reliably measure between collector and emitter because of the nature of the transistor. A bipolar transistor is like two diodes placed together. When you measure between the base and emitter in one direction, you will get a reading like a regular diode—about 500 ohms. If you reverse the leads, the DMM will measure infinite resistance. The same between the base and collector. A bad transistor, like a bad diode, will measure either a short or open in both directions.

Sometimes, a transistor has a built-in bias resistor between the base and emitter. This will cause you to get a low reading of approximately 160 to 180 ohms, due to the

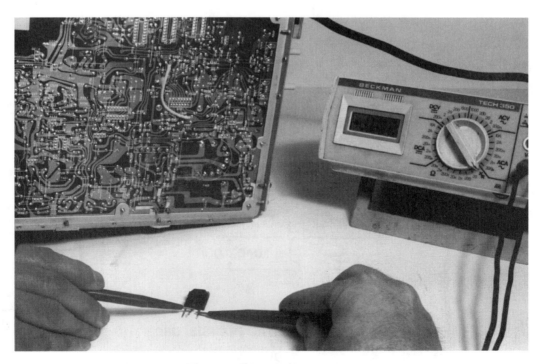

Figure 5.5. Measuring the resistance between the base and the collector of a transistor.

resistor that is there. If you suspect this is the case, you must check out the part in a reference such as the ECG Semiconductors Master Replacement Guide from Philips ECG. This cross-reference manual will tell you if a transistor has a built-in resistor (see **Figure 5.6**). Also, the schematic of the monitor sometimes shows this built-in bias resistor. If the transistor does not have a built-in resistor for a bias yet still has a low reading, the transistor is leaky and has to be replaced

You can check ICs (with a DMM on the diode setting) only for a short. You cannot check if the IC is good or bad because of the complexity of the integrated circuit. But, you can check for a short, for example, between the supply voltage (Vcc) and ground pins. Most ICs have a built-in regulator at the Vcc pin. If there is a short, you can be fairly certain the IC is bad. If there is no short, the IC may or may not be good. A reliable way of checking integrated cir-

cuits with common test equipment doesn't exist. There are some specialized gadgets that check ICs, but even these don't check every type of IC.

If you measure a short between Vcc and ground, then you should disconnect the pin of the IC from the printed circuit board. You can do this by desoldering the pin with the solder sucker until all solder is removed from the pin. You do not have to remove the IC from the PC board. Simply make sure that the one pin in question (Vcc) is completely disconnected from the PC board. Once this is done, you have to make the measurement again. If you measure a short again, the IC has to be replaced.

Shorts in ICs do not always occur between Vcc and ground. On some ICs, such as the vertical output IC, the short normally occurs between the Vcc and the output. Again, you can check the two pins for a dead short but nothing else.

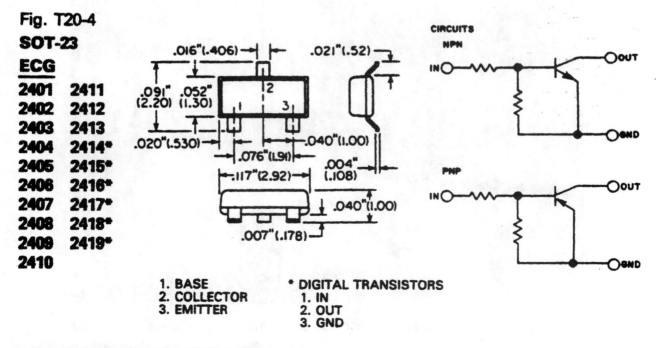

Figure 5.6. A transistor with a built-in bias resistor.

You do not always need a DMM to determine whether a resistor, diode or transistor is shorted or open. Sometimes, you can do it by inspection. For example, if you notice that a resistor is clearly burned out (see **Figure 5.7**), you can be sure it is open. All you have to do (instead of measuring it) is check the colors of the resistor. This is necessary to find a suitable replacement. If the resistor is burned so badly that you cannot figure out the value, you'll have to purchase the service manual for the monitor.

If a resistor or any other component has burned out, chances are the circuitry following the burned component is destroyed, too. In fact, this circuitry probably caused the component to burn out in the first place.

So, any time you see a burned resistor, you have to check the components connected to that resistor, like transistors, regulators, and integrated circuits.

Figure 5.7. A burned resistor.

Chapter 6
Practical Repair Techniques

Repairing a computer monitor is not just a matter of finding the source of the problem and replacing the defective part. Any repair starts with disassembly of the monitor. You may think this simply means removing the rear cover of the monitor. With very old monitors, this may be true. Modern day monitors, however, have heavy shielding to comply with industry safety standards. In this chapter, we cover the steps typically needed—over and above the troubleshooting process—to complete the repair.

6.1 Disassembly and Re-assembly

The disassembly needed to arrive at the point where you can start troubleshooting varies from monitor to monitor. Some monitors are completely shielded. Essentially, these monitors have a metal cabinet inside the outer plastic cabinet. It's as difficult to make measurements through the metal cabinet as it is through the plastic cabinet. Some monitors are partially shielded. For these monitors, you may or may not be able to make measurements, depending on where the shields are. Most certainly, though, you will have to do some serious disassembly to get at the foil side of any of the PC boards.

We will cover one disassembly scenario in detail to give you a good idea of what is involved. The Magnavox Model 6CM320974I is completely shielded in a metal enclosure (see **Figure 6.1**). In order to work on this chassis, you have to remove all parts of the enclosure. An electric screwdriver is a very handy tool for this job. As you remove the right and left metal sides, you have to disconnect the controls from the main circuit board at the

Figure 6.1. When you remove the rear cover, you can see that the Magnavox 6CM320974I is completely shielded in a metal enclosure.

bottom of the monitor and the power switch from the power supply. Naturally, you cannot turn on the monitor without these parts. So, you have to disengage the controls and the power switch from the metal sides (see **Figure 6.2** and **Figure 6.3**) and reattach them to the monitor. Once the top and two sides of the shield are removed, you can slide the main PC board out from the bottom shield (see **Figure 6.4**). This gives you access to the foil side of the main board.

In the case of the Magnavox, we found that it could not support itself once the metal shield was removed. We were fearful that any little slip would damage the neck of the CRT. This would be a disaster! We solved the support problem by screwing metal rods to the sides of the front part of the plastic cabinet in the same screw holes used by the metal sides of the shield (see **Figure 6.5**). This gave the chassis the support it needed when the monitor was in the upright position (see **Figure 6.6**). In other positions, on its side or with the CRT face down on the bench, support from the metal rods was not needed.

Disassembly often involves removing wires that connect the various PC boards together. If you don't have a good memory, you may want to note on a piece of paper which wires go where and in what orientation.

Disassembly sometimes means disconnecting the circuits of the monitor from the CRT. To do this, you must disconnect the socket, which is attached to a small PC board, from the neck of the CRT (see **Figure 6.7**). You need to exercise great care when doing this so as not to damage the neck of the picture tube. You may also have to remove the anode cap from the CRT. Before trying to do this, you must first follow the safety precautions outlined in Chapter 4.

To remove the anode cap, you have to understand what is underneath it. The cap covers the wire coming from the flyback transformer. At the end of this wire is a "clip" that looks like two L-shaped wires facing away from each other. These wires fit into a small hole in the CRT. To remove the cap, you have to push the clip to one side, squeeze the ends of the clip together, and pull it out of the CRT. You have to push the clip together with some force to get it out (see **Figure 6.8**).

Re-assembly of the monitor is, obviously, the opposite of disassembly. Re-assembly requires that you remember all the steps involved in disassembly, which is sometimes difficult to do. Again, use as much backup material as you need, in terms of drawings and diagrams or even Polaroid photos, to assist in the re-assembly process.

It is not uncommon, during disassembly and re-assembly, to break off a wire or otherwise damage the monitor. When you put the monitor back into operation, you may find a problem different from the original one. For example, if you break off a wire going to the CRT board, you may find that the monitor is missing a color when you perform the final checkout. Don't despair if this is the case. You are probably not looking at a major repair, but more likely just soldering a wire back into place.

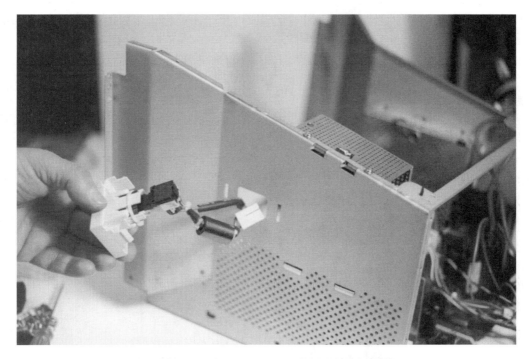

Figure 6.3. Disengaging the power switch from the metal shield.

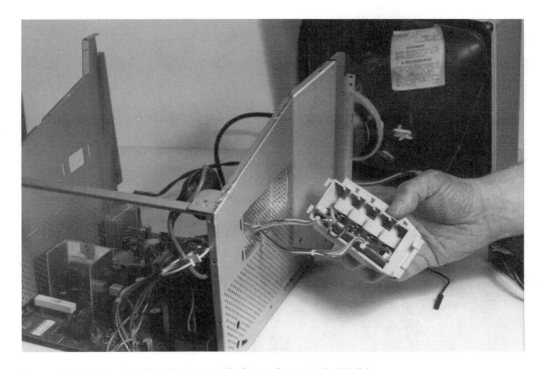

Figure 6.2. Disengaging the controls from the metal shield.

Figure 6.4. Sliding out the main PC board from the bottom shield of the monitor.

Figure 6.5. We screwed metal rods to the sides of the monitor for support.

Figure 6.6. The metal rods support the monitor when in the upright position.

Figure 6.7. Disconnecting the socket from the neck of the CRT.

Figure 6.8. Removing the anode cap (don't try this unless you have removed the power cord from the monitor and grounded the anode as described in Chapter 4).

6.2 Handling the Monitor

When a computer monitor first arrives on the bench, it is upright and probably resting on a pedestal. When you repair a monitor, you have to "knock it off its pedestal" in a sense. You will have to remove the pedestal, remove the rear part of the cabinet, and very likely remove most of the metal shielding in order to get at the monitor's PC boards.

Once you have the monitor open, don't be afraid to turn it on its side or upside down. You may even place the monitor right on its face (see **Figure 6.9**), if it helps you get at the component or circuit you want to check. Of course, you must always be careful not to break the neck or otherwise damage the CRT.

Also, don't be afraid to pull out PC boards and turn them around if you need to. You should try not to break wires that connect one board to another. But even if you do, these breaks are usually easy to repair. Remember, the more access you have to the computer monitor circuits, the better able you will be to make measurements and repairs.

6.3 Replacing Components

Replacing components is a straightforward job if the monitor has a standard printed circuit board and standard components, in other words, no surface mount devices. Once you gain experience, removing solder with a solder sucker or a solder wick is relatively easy. You remove the solder from the leads of the component, and the component comes out very easily. You should

Figure 6.9. You may place the monitor on its face (very carefully) if this helps you get to the component or circuit you want to check.

not exert force to remove components; this can easily damage them.

Integrated circuits are more difficult to remove than components such as diodes and transistors, since they have more leads. A microprocessor, for example, typically has 60 or more leads. But, you can remove ICs the same way you remove other components. Simply remove the solder from all the pins of the IC and then pry it out of the PC board, usually with a small flathead screwdriver. Again, do not exert any unreasonable force. If an IC is completely desoldered, it will come out without too much effort on your part.

Sometimes, components have a mechanical attachment to the PC board in addition to the solder. This occurs during the manufacturing process when a component's leads are bent after insertion into the holes on the PC board. You may have to use a

small screwdriver or a long-nose pliers to undo the mechanical bond while you are melting the solder with an iron.

Desoldering electronic components demands good coordination. You will be holding a soldering iron in one hand and a solder sucker in the other (see **Figure 6.10**). Solder suckers are usually spring loaded, which means you have to press a spring to get them ready to suck the solder. Then, you have to release the spring at the proper time—just as the solder is melting. To do the job right, it helps immensely to have the printed circuit board in a convenient position for desoldering. This means you have to maneuver the monitor into position as described in the previous section.

You need to bring your soldering skills up to a certain level before you can become proficient doing repair work. If you are

Figure 6.10. Desoldering a component requires holding a soldering iron in one hand and a solder sucker in the other.

having difficulty with the desoldering and resoldering process, you should practice on older electronic equipment, for which you no longer have any use.

Surface mount devices are a different breed of component. First, you have to use a solder wick to release the solder. Then, you have to pry the component from the printed circuit board, because it is glued to the board at the factory. The glue is used to hold components before they are soldered in place.

To insert a new component, you need to place a little bit of glue on its side. Once you glue the component in place, you solder it using a very small soldering iron and a small amount of solder.

Surface mount integrated circuits are more difficult to remove and replace. These tiny

ICs have pins on all four sides. In order to release the solder on all the rows of pins simultaneously, you need a special soldering iron that is shaped like the IC. The iron is placed on top of the IC and it desolders all of pins at the same time with a vacuum pump action.

These tools are quite expensive and mostly used in factories and service centers that do rework on printed circuit boards. Another way to remove surface mount ICs is by removing the solder with a solder wick very carefully and then prying them up with a small flathead screwdriver. You have to do this very carefully so as not to break the copper traces. The traces are very thin and very easy to break.

Replacing surface mount devices is a time consuming and difficult operation. You should not even attempt to do it unless you have some experience. How do you gain experience? Practice, of course. If you have some old electronics equipment (not too old) such as a personal stereo or a TV (the tuner section), you can practice soldering and desolding all the surface mount parts.

6.4 Repairing Cracked Solder Joints and PC Boards

Cracked or broken solder joints can completely disable a computer monitor. The cracks may occur themselves, in which case you have to track them down. Or, you may inadvertently break a joint or pad during the course of a repair.

Simple cracks and cold solder joints can be repaired by melting the old solder with an iron and adding a bit of new solder to the joint (see **Figure 6.11**). More involved

cracks, possibly of a pad or trace, are best fixed by soldering a jumper wire to the PC board. The jumper wire takes the place of the broken or cracked pad or trace.

If a PC board cracks for some reason—possibly the monitor fell on the floor—it can usually be repaired. The proper way to do this is to first glue the pieces of the board back together. When the glue dries and the board is back in one piece, you have to scrape the conformal coating off of the broken traces on the PC board. You can do this with a sharp tool, such as an X-Acto™ knife. Then, you have to solder a jumper wire to connect the broken pieces of the trace. If traces are very close together, you have to be very careful that jumper wires don't touch each other and that solder doesn't create a bridge between adjacent traces.

Figure 6.11. Simple cracks and cold solder joints can be repaired by melting the old solder with an iron and adding a bit of new solder to the joint.

Chapter 7

Determining the Problem

When a monitor first comes in for repair, you should try to get as much information as possible from the customer. If the customer tells you the monitor is dead, you should ask when and how it happened. You might find out about an electrical storm or some other condition that will point you right to the source of the problem—before removing the cover of the monitor.

Always keep in mind that a monitor is a part of the personal computer *system*. Although the customer may perceive a problem with the monitor, there may be nothing at all wrong with it. The problem may lie with the graphics adapter or with the operating system software. This is why a computer monitor pattern generator is an important piece of test equipment to own. If the customer brings in the complete system, you can isolate the problem right away. Simply disconnect the monitor from the computer and connect the monitor to the pattern generator.

Once you have determined that the problem resides in the monitor and have listened to the complaints of the customer, you should verify those complaints while the customer is still at the repair shop. If the customer tells you the monitor is dead, make sure this is the case. If the customer complains about the brightness, make sure that the problem cannot be fixed by simply turning up the brightness control. Once you are satisfied that there is a legitimate problem and have discussed the financial terms of the repair, you are ready to begin the troubleshooting phase of the repair.

7.1 Preliminary Troubleshooting

After you place the monitor on the bench, the first thing to do is check the condition of the monitor. Check to see if there is any obvious damage. Check the AC power cord and cable that connects to the computer. If everything looks okay, connect the monitor to a computer (or computer monitor pattern generator) and turn everything on.

After a short warm-up period of about thirty seconds, the monitor should display an image or a pattern. Sometimes, the monitor will be completely dead. If this is the case, disconnect the computer and prepare to remove the rear cover of the monitor. Other times, the monitor will operate, but not in the proper way. Check to see if all the controls are working. Check to see if the picture is overscanned or underscanned. Check for all of the colors. Check the focus. Check to see if the picture is excessively bright or dark.

All this preliminary checking from the outside helps to determine the problem inside the monitor. Once you finish your external inspection and decide there is a problem with the monitor, it is time to begin disassembly of the monitor.

Disassembly begins by removing the tilt-and-swivel stand, a standard fixture on most monitors. Then, you take the back cover off. This usually entails removing a few screws (see **Figure 7.1**). As mentioned earlier, in many of the newer monitors, not only do you have to take off the back cover, you also have to remove one or more shields that surround the picture tube and circuitry. The shields are there to protect

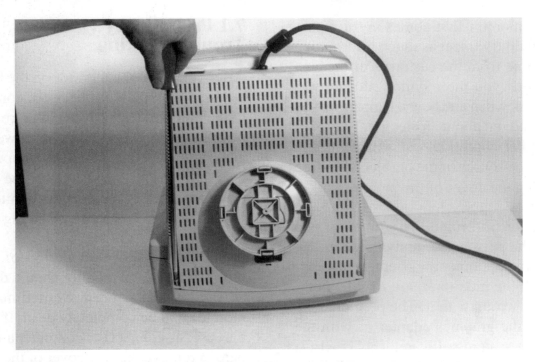

Figure 7.1. To remove the back cover of the monitor, you have to remove several screws.

people who are using the monitor and also to protect anyone who may be working in close proximity to the monitor. The shield helps to block harmful radiation from being emitted from the monitor's CRT.

Once you remove the shield, which usually takes some time, you will have a good view of the printed circuit boards inside the monitor. A typical monitor has a main board, which contains the horizontal and vertical sync circuits, a power supply board, a video board, and a small board attached to the neck of the CRT.

You should examine each printed circuit board closely to make sure it is not cracked or broken. A monitor may fall off a desk, and one of the printed circuit boards may crack. If the board is cracked, you may be able to repair it with the techniques described in the previous chapter. If the crack

is beyond repair, there is nothing you can do. You have to replace the whole printed circuit board, which can be quite a job.

Also, during your examination of the printed circuit board you should look for cracked solder joints, burned resistors, blown capacitors or diodes, or anything else visible to the naked eye. A burned resistor may be completely charred or have just a burn mark on it (see **Figure 7.2**). A blown electrolytic capacitor may be bursting at the seams or have its insides sticking out of the top of the can. A blown diode may be cracked or missing altogether! Any one of these conditions is a strong clue as to the source of the problem. Most likely, there is a short circuited component such as a transistor or IC in the area where the burned or blown part resides.

Figure 7.2. A burned resistor may be completely charred or have just a burn mark on it.

One last component to check, usually on the main PC board, is the high-voltage transformer, also know as the flyback transformer (see **Figure 7.3**). You may notice cracks or melted plastic. This indicates that the transformer is bad and should be replaced. If this is the case, you should unplug the monitor and replace the transformer.

If the PC board and components look okay—nothing is burned or damaged—it is time to power up the monitor. The first thing to do when you power up is to examine the neck of the picture tube. See if the picture tube filament is lit. If it is, this indicates that the high-voltage circuits are working. If the filament is not lit, then the problem resides either with the high-voltage circuits or the power supply.

7.2 Checking the High-Voltage Section

The high-voltage section of a monitor includes the horizontal output transistor and the flyback transformer. It is easy to find the horizontal output transistor; it is mounted on a heat sink located near the flyback transformer (see **Figure 7.4**). You have to check to see if this transistor is getting power.

Normally, the voltage is between 80 and 100 volts DC at the collector of the horizontal output transistor. If that voltage is there, and the filament of the picture tube is not lit, chances are that the drive circuits are not working. In other words, the horizontal output transistor is getting power, but the base of this transistor is not being driven by the horizontal driver transistor. This problem arises if the leads of

Figure 7.3. The flyback transformer on the main board of a computer monitor.

Figure 7.4. The horizontal output transistor is usually mounted on a heat sink located near the flyback transformer.

the driver transistor or transformer become loose or the solder joints break. We'll go into the details of this problem later on in the book.

7.3 Checking the Power Supply

If the power is not there when you measure at the collector of the horizontal output transistor, then you have to check the power supply circuits. Most computer monitors use a switch mode power supply, which is complex but not that difficult to check out or repair.

Sometimes, the power supply of a computer monitor is physically separate from the main PC board (see **Figure 7.5**); sometimes, the circuitry is built right onto the main board (see **Figure 7.6**).

If you suspect that the power supply is not producing any power, it is a good idea to disconnect it from the AC power line. After a few seconds, discharge all the large capacitors with a screwdriver. Then, measure with a DMM on the diode setting to find out if there are any shorts in the power supply.

The power supply is actually connected to the monitor's chassis. If you make a measurement in the power supply, you are actually measuring the rest of the chassis. Let's say that a switch mode power supply has three outputs that supply three different voltages. If you check for shorts at the three capacitors that filter the voltage coming from the transformer, and you don't find any, chances are there are no shorts in the chassis of the computer monitor. If you notice that one of the capacitors measures short, then either the capacitor is shorted

out or the circuitry that connects to that filter has a short.

If the monitor has a power supply that is physically separate from the rest of the circuitry, then you may disconnect it and test it as a separate unit. This is not always a reliable test, though. Some power supplies produce problems only when connected to a load. If you test the supply without a load, it may test good. But, when it is connected to the chassis, the voltage may drop down dramatically, indicating a problem in the power supply.

If the power supply resides on the main PC board, you cannot separate it from the rest of the monitor's circuitry. In this case, you will have to check the supply dynamically to find out which voltages are there and which are missing.

It may happen that the power supply is good, but because of a short in the chassis, the supply is in a shutdown condition. In other words, it is not producing any power due to a short in the main circuitry. In this case, you will have to find the short and repair whatever is causing it, either a transistor or an IC.

7.4 Checking the Monitor Controls

Your preliminary examination of the monitor may lead you to conclude that one or more monitor controls are not working. Most monitors have both external and internal controls. External controls, such as brightness and contrast, are meant to be adjusted by the user. Internals controls, such as horizontal hold, are preset by the manufacturer and meant to be adjusted

Figure 7.5. Some computer monitor power supplies are physically separate from the main PC board.

Figure 7.6. Some power supplies are built right onto the main board of the computer monitor.

only by a service technician. Internal controls (potentiometers) are typically mounted on the printed circuit board. **Figure 7.7** shows the external controls of the Magnavox 6CM320974I as well as the access holes at the bottom right for adjusting the internal controls. **Figure 7.8** shows the internal controls on the PC board.

How can you tell if there is a problem with an internal control? Turn the control (usually with a screwdriver placed into a slot on the control). If the display does not change, the control is not working. For example, if you turn the pincushion control, you should see the display curve out or in. If nothing happens, it may be the fault of the control itself or, more likely, the circuitry to which that control is attached.

The value of a control is normally marked right on it with numbers. For example, a potentiometer marked 203 has a value of 20,000 ohms or 20 K. The last number indicates the number of zeros, in this case three, which means 20 plus three zeros or 20,000. You can very easily measure the value of a potentiometer by using a DMM set to measure ohms.

Before you take the measurement, you should desolder the control from the PC board. Place the leads of the ohmmeter between the two ends of the control. If the DMM measures 20 plus or minus the tolerance, which is usually 10%, the control is in good shape. Next, measure from one end of the control to the center and turn it slowly with a screwdriver to see if the resistance changes. If the resistance changes gradually (no drastic jumps up or down) the control is considered good. Before you

resolder the control to the PC board, it is a good idea to spray the control with contact cleaner or a light lubricant. Over the years, dust accumulates between the slider and the contact surface of the control and can cause the control to lose its function. Even if the control checks out okay, cleaning it is a good preventive measure.

If you find that the potentiometer is in good working condition, but the control function still does not operate, then the problem lies with the circuitry for that control. A very good example of this type of problem is given in the case studies of this book.

External controls may also cause problems. If a monitor has rotary controls, it is always a good idea to spray the controls with contact cleaner, lubricate them with a light oil, and check all the connections that go to the printed circuit board. After years of operation, the solder may crack where the control connects to the PC board. This causes erratic operation of the control.

Some newer monitors have digital controls. With digital controls, an external pushbutton switch is used to vary the control (see **Figure 7.9**). If the monitor does not have an on-screen display, pushing the control will vary the look of the display. If there is an on-screen display, the current value of the control will appear on the screen. In either case, if you do not get a response when you push the control button, the switch may be defective. In this case, you would have to clean or replace the switch.

Also, with digital controls, one of the switches may get stuck for one reason or

Figure 7.7. The external controls of the Magnavox 6CM320974I (top) and the access holes for adjusting the internal controls (bottom right).

Figure 7.8. The internal controls on the main PC board of the Magnavox 6CM320974I.

another. When one control gets stuck, it is not unusual for nothing else to work. You may not even be able to turn the monitor on and off. If you suspect a problem with the controls, you should press each one until you hear a distinctive click. If you don't hear the click, the button is no good and should be replaced.

Figure 7.9. Digital controls are pushbutton switches available to the user.

Chapter 8
Troubleshooting High-Voltage Circuits

Let's begin this chapter by addressing the question of why a monitor needs high voltage. The monitor is an output device for the computer. In effect, the monitor shows the user what's going on inside the computer. The monitor's primary source of display is the CRT, the so-called cathode ray tube. The CRT is a large glass tube whose inner front surface is covered with a phosphorus material. An electron gun at the back of the tube shoots electrons to the front of the tube. When electrons strike the phosphorus material, light is emitted. Through control of the position and intensity of the electron beam, the monitor can display text and graphics in any color imaginable. In this way, the user is able to see the information contained in the computer.

The electrons inside the picture tube must be accelerated to a point where they can hit the phosphors in the front of the picture tube hard enough to produce light. Acceleration is accomplished with a high voltage produced by the monitor. The level of this voltage varies from one monitor to another depending on the size of the CRT. On a 14" monitor, the high voltage may be 20,000 volts; on a larger monitor, the voltage may be 30,000 volts or more. Larger CRTs need higher voltages to accelerate the electron beam due to the increased distance the electron must travel inside the picture tube before it hits the phosphorus material.

8.1 Checking the Horizontal Output Transistor

Percentage-wise, most monitor repairs involve the high-voltage section. It's not an exaggeration to say that 80% of the trouble in monitors comes from the high-voltage section. Why? All the parts in the high-voltage section are highly stressed. For example, the horizontal output transistor, which switches the flyback transformer and produces the high voltage, is the most stressed part in the monitor.

To check if the high voltage is present, take a quick look at the filament in the neck of the picture tube. If the filament is glowing orange, the high voltage is present. If the filament is not lit, then there may be a problem with the high voltage. The first thing to do in a case like this is to check the horizontal output transistor. **Figure 8.1** shows the horizontal output transistor of the Magnavox 6CM320974I monitor. **Figure 8.2** shows the schematic diagram of the high-voltage section. The horizontal output transistor is labeled 7409.

To check the horizontal output transistor, first disconnect the power from the monitor. Then, with the DMM on the diode setting, check if the output transistor is shorted out. If it is, it must be replaced. You can get lucky with this kind of repair. You simply replace the blown transistor and the problem is solved. After all, as we have already stated, this transistor is a highly stressed component. It may short out on its own, for no apparent reason. It is not good repair practice, though, to simply replace a shorted component and then power up the monitor. You should try to determine *why* the transistor shorted out.

If another component caused the horizontal output transistor to short out, replacing the transistor will not solve the problem. The source of the problem lies somewhere else. One place to look is the switch mode

Figure 8.1. The horizontal output transistor of the Magnavox 6CM320974I monitor.

power supply. A switch mode power supply may go out of control, especially the feedback circuit of the power supply. If this happens, the supply voltage increases and eventually destroys the output transistor. The excessive voltage increases the current to the transistor and it goes beyond the specifications that the transistor can handle.

With this in mind, here is the proper way to replace a shorted horizontal output transistor. First, remove the transistor from the PC board. To do this, desolder the three legs of the transistor, remove the screw that attaches the transistor's tab to the heat sink (if there is one), and take out the transistor. Then, with the horizontal output transistor out of the circuit, power up the monitor and measure the DC voltage at the point where the collector connects to the circuit. If the voltage is within specs (according to the service manual) the power supply is probably okay. But, this is still a quick judgment. Power supplies often develop problems after they warm up slightly. The supply may take fifteen or twenty minutes to warm up. Then, the voltage starts increasing. Instead of, for example, the voltage being at 100 volts, it gradually increases to 105, 110 and eventually destroys the output transistor. Thus, it is a good idea to let the power supply warm up completely before making a determination about whether or not it is functioning properly. Taking voltage measurements at regular intervals during a 30-minute period will provide the information you need to make the correct decision about the supply.

If the power supply checks out okay, you may replace the output transistor without fear that it will blow out again, either right away or after a short period of time. It is always a good idea to replace the horizontal output transistor with an exact replace-

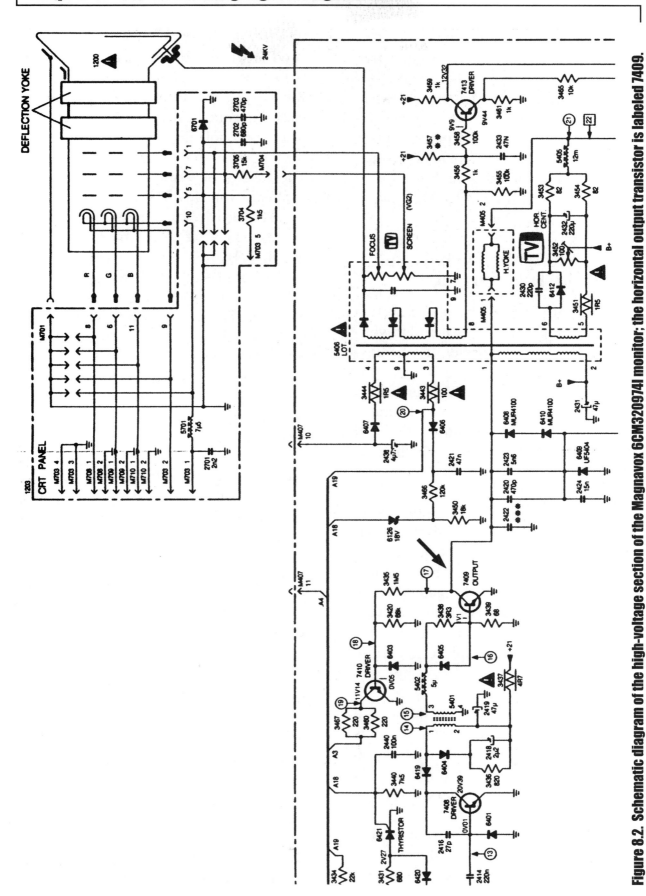

Figure 8.2. Schematic diagram of the high-voltage section of the Magnavox 6CM3209741 monitor; the horizontal output transistor is labeled 7409.

ment part. Generic parts work okay, too, but it's best to stick with the original part. You will save yourself time and trouble. To obtain an original part you may have to call the manufacturer, but this is not always necessary. You can call any parts supplier, because these transistors are not manufactured by the company that makes the monitor. Most monitor makers buy the transistors from suppliers.

8.2 Checking the High-Voltage (Flyback) Transformer

Another part of the high-voltage section that can cause problems is the high-voltage or flyback transformer. This transformer is a so-called integrated high-voltage transformer (IHVT). The term *integrated* means that in addition to the transformer, the device has built-in rectifiers and divider networks. In **Figure 8.2**, the area surrounded by the dotted line represents the flyback transformer. Notice the rectifiers and resistor networks in this area. In effect, the high-voltage transformer contains three separate circuits that work together. You cannot separate these circuits because they are molded together in the manufacturing process. Let's say one of the rectifiers is shorted out. You cannot fix this problem; you have to replace the entire unit.

The rectifier in a flyback transformer is a so-called voltage tripler. Years ago, this part was separate from the transformer, so you could replace only the tripler if it shorted out. But today, with the one-piece construction, it is not worth the effort to measure whether the rectifiers are good or not (there are ways to do this), since you cannot replace them. A sure sign that ei-

ther the transformer or rectifiers are no good is when the horizontal output transistor gets very hot after a few minutes. But, it doesn't matter which part of the flyback has gone bad, since you have to replace the whole thing.

The resistor networks control the screen and focus voltages. The bottom control on the flyback is always the screen control, the top one is the focus control (see **Figure 8.3**). By adjusting the screen control (see **Figure 8.4**), you can bring the screen brightness to a normal level, about 400 to 450 volts. The screen voltage is the G2 grid on the CRT. Note, these adjustments can be made without removing the shield of a computer monitor. **Figure 8.5** shows the cutouts in the metal shield of the Magnavox monitor for making these adjustments.

It is best to adjust the focus when you have a pattern on the screen. Using a pattern that fills the screen with the lower case letter "m" or the number "4" helps you to make the proper adjustment (see **Figure 8.6**). When you fine tune the focus, you get the most out of the resolution of the monitor.

Both the focus and screen controls can burn out due to bad contacts. For example, you might find that you adjust the focus, and then, a few days later, the focus goes out of whack again. If you experience problems with either control, you have no other choice but to replace the high-voltage transformer. These controls are not replaceable. This is not a usual occurrence, but it does happen.

Replacing the flyback transformer is a straightforward and relatively easy pro-

Figure 8.3. The bottom control on the flyback is always the screen control, the top one is the focus control.

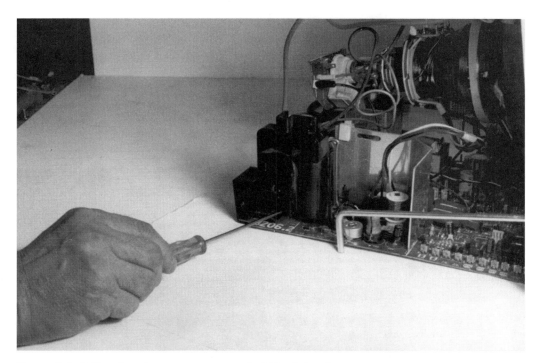

Figure8.4. Adjusting the screen control of the flyback transformer.

Figure 8.5. Cutouts in the metal shield of the Magnavox monitor for the focus and screen controls of the flyback transformer.

Figure 8.6. A typical pattern used when adjusting the focus.

cess, which is done with the power cord removed from the monitor and the anode grounded as explained in Chapter 4. The first thing you have to do is desolder all the leads going from the flyback transformer to the printed circuit board (see **Figure 8.7**). You should use a quality soldering iron, about 30 watts, and a solder sucker or a solder wick, whichever you prefer. Clean the solder off all the leads so they are free from the hole (there is no more solder to hold them). Next, you have to check the mechanical connection between the flyback and the PC board. Some flybacks are attached to the printed circuit board with screws, usually two or four. Some don't have screws, but use plastic clips instead. These clips click into square cutouts in the printed circuit board to keep the transformer in place. Once the solder is removed from all the leads, all you have to do is remove the screws if the flyback is

held on with screws, or press in the plastic clips that lock the transformer onto the PC board. The transformer will come out very easily (see **Figure 8.8**).

To finish the job, you need to disconnect three wires that run from the flyback to other parts of the monitor. First is the focus wire. Typically, this wire goes to the third grid of the picture tube socket. Sometimes the connection is protected by a hinged cover. If it is there, you have to open the cover and desolder the focus lead (see **Figure 8.9**). Second is the screen voltage wire. This goes to the printed circuit board at the picture tube socket. This needs to be desoldered, too (see **Figure 8.10**). Finally, you have to unhook the high voltage lead that goes to the anode terminal of the picture tube. Normally, this wire ends in a spring-loaded clip. You have to push the clip to one side so that one pin is released,

Figure 8.7. Desoldering the leads at the base of the flyback transformer.

Figure 8.8. Removing the flyback transformer.

Figure 8.9. Removing the focus lead of the flyback from the PC board.

Figure 8.10. Removing the screen lead of the flyback from the PC board.

Figure 8.11. Removing the anode lead of the flyback from the anode terminal of the CRT.

and then you push it to the other side and pull it up (see **Figure 8.11**). Once you release these three wires, you can remove the old flyback.

When you remove the old flyback from the monitor, it's a good idea to check the printed circuit board for burn spots. Sometimes the transformer burns and damages the printed circuit board. Burn spots are conductive. If you put in the new transformer, you may have a problem. If you see a burn spot, you should scrape it with a razor blade, a sharp screwdriver, or a scraper. Scrape the burn spot until you reach a clean surface. Also, before you reinstall the transformer, apply a high-voltage putty or silicone (silicone from General Electric is a very good one) to the area before you put the new transformer on the printed circuit board. Silicone offers a very good isolation for the high voltage.

When you put in the new flyback transformer, make sure all the pins are aligned properly. Then, push it down and solder all the pins with the soldering iron. Make sure to make rounded, shiny solder connections. You don't want to create cold solder joints, which appear as dull blobs of solder. Once the flyback is soldered properly and secured, you must reconnect the three wires. Solder in place the two wires for the screen and focus voltages and then install the high-voltage clip into the anode of the picture tube. This completes the process.

Please read the chapter on safety considerations before you attempt to do anything with the picture tube. As mentioned, the picture tube is like a giant capacitor. Even though the monitor may not have been powered for several days, it may still hold a heavy charge. The moment you try to pull the anode lead from the picture tube, you may get a nasty shock. So before you do that, it's a must to ground the anode as described in Chapter 4. Then, there is no more voltage, there is no more danger, and you can do the repair.

Chapter 9
Troubleshooting Horizontal Circuits

In order for the electron beam inside of the picture tube to make a sensible picture, it has to be deflected from the point of origin. In other words, when an electron is emitted from the cathode of the picture tube, it tends to travel straight ahead until it hits the phosphor on the face of the CRT. This behavior, however, would simply create a dot in the middle of the screen. Instead, the beam of electrons has to be deflected up and down (vertically) and left and right (horizontally).

The most common type of deflection used in a picture tube is the magnetic field deflection. This is accomplished with a coil, called a yoke, that surrounds the neck of the picture tube. One part of the yoke is used for horizontal deflection and the other part for vertical deflection. The horizontal circuits energize the horizontal deflection yoke, while the vertical circuits do the same for the vertical deflection yoke.

In this chapter, we explain the horizontal circuits, whose primary role is to deflect the beam from left to right in a horizontal plane. The horizontal circuits consist of the horizontal oscillator, horizontal driver circuits, and horizontal output circuits, as well as the horizontal controls for sync, phase, linearity, position and width. These circuits typically reside on the main PC board in a computer monitor (see **Figure 9.1**).

9.1 Horizontal Sync Signal

A horizontal sync signal comes into the monitor at pin 13 of the 15-pin connector at the rear of the monitor or end of the video signal cable. This signal (see **Figure 9.2**) is simply a pulse waveform. It is devel-

Figure 9.1. The horizontal circuits on the main PC board of the NEC Multisync 4D. The horizontal output transistor is attached to the large heat sink; the horizontal oscillator chip is to the right.

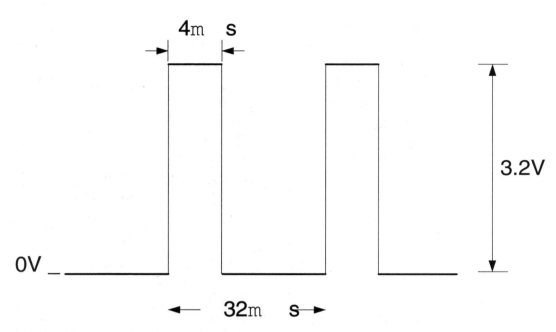

Figure 9.2. The horizontal sync signal.

oped on the video adapter inside the computer. The frequency of the horizontal sync depends on the video mode selected by the user. For example, if the user selects 640 x 480 VGA mode, the horizontal sync signal typically has a frequency of 31.5 kHz; if the user selects 800 x 600 SVGA mode, the horizontal sync signal may have a frequency of 35.1 kHz. The signal has standard transistor-transistor levels (TTL) (LOW = 0 to 0.8 volts; HIGH = 2.4 to 5 volts) and may have a positive or negative polarity, which is dependent on the video mode selected. The purpose of the horizontal sync signal is to control the horizontal oscillator so that it runs at the required frequency.

9.2 The Horizontal Oscillator

The horizontal oscillator creates a signal that drives the horizontal driver and horizontal output circuits to produce the horizontal deflection for the electron beam in the picture tube and high voltage for the anode of the picture tube. The frequency

of the horizontal oscillator is controlled by the horizontal sync signal.

In the Magnavox 6CM320974I monitor, the horizontal oscillator is part of IC7406 (see **Figure 9.3**). The IC contains a generator, phase detector, voltage stabilizer and an amplifier. The horizontal sync pulse enters the IC at pin 7. The output of the IC is pin 1, which feeds the horizontal driver circuits.

In the NEC Multisync 4D monitor, the horizontal oscillator is part of IC501 (see **Figure 9.4**) . The generic part number is LA7853. This IC actually contains the horizontal and vertical oscillators. The horizontal sync signal enters the IC at pin 21. The horizontal output is at pin 13, which feeds the horizontal driver circuits.

In the Samtron SC-728SXL monitor, the horizontal oscillator is IC302 (see **Figure 9.5**). The generic part number is TDA9102. The horizontal sync signal enters the IC at

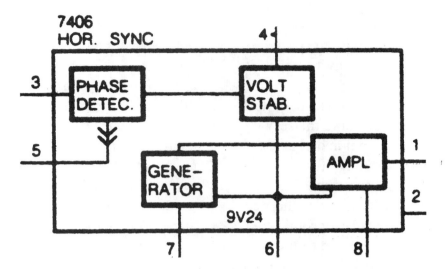

Figure 9.3. In the Magnavox 6CM320974I monitor, the horizontal oscillator is part of IC7406.

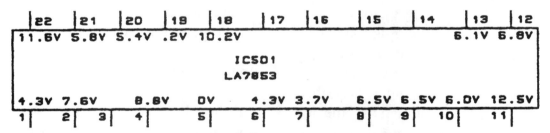

Figure 9.4. In the NEC Multisync 4D monitor, the horizontal oscillator is part of IC501.

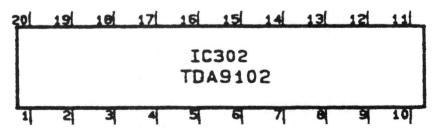

Figure 9.5. In the Samtron SC-728SXL monitor, the horizontal oscillator is IC302.

pin 4. The horizontal output is at pin 6, which feeds the horizontal driver circuits.

If you suspect a problem with the horizontal oscillator, there is no way to check it with a DMM to find out if it is good or bad. We have a simple way to check the horizontal oscillator IC. Using the service manual, locate the Vcc pin and check the voltage at that pin. Normally, it is between 12 and 15 volts. Then, from a bench power supply, hook up the positive lead to the Vcc pin and the negative lead to ground and supply the appropriate voltage to the pin. If the oscillator is working, it will produce a signal at the output, which you can monitor with an oscilloscope. If the output is good and the peak-to-peak voltage is within specifications as shown in the service manual, then the IC is good. If you don't have the service manual for a particular monitor, you may want to check the *ECG Replacement Guide* or any other IC master book to find out the functions of the pins. Once you find the pinout, apply the voltage to the proper pin as described above. This is a dynamic test of the IC, which is very reliable.

The horizontal IC is usually connected to a shutdown circuit. When there is excessive high voltage, this circuit shuts down the horizontal oscillator. When the horizontal oscillator shuts down, there is no drive signal for the horizontal output transistor and, therefore, no display on the monitor.

9.3 Horizontal Drive Circuits

The horizontal drive circuits consist of a horizontal drive transistor connected to a horizontal drive transformer. Why do you need these circuits? Why can't the horizontal oscillator drive the horizontal output transistor directly? The horizontal output transistor normally is a bipolar NPN transistor, which has a low input impedance from base to ground. In order to drive this kind of transistor, the circuit has to provide the necessary current. Meanwhile, the horizontal oscillator has a high-impedance output. If you connect the two together, the horizontal oscillator will not produce anything. The low input impedance of the output transistor will shunt the oscillator output to ground.

To avoid this, designers connect a high-input impedance transistor, such as a MOSFET, to the output of the horizontal oscillator IC. Then, a horizontal drive transformer converts the voltage gain of the driver transistor at its primary to current at its secondary. The secondary of the driver transformer has a very low impedance, which can drive the horizontal output transistor.

In the Magnavox 6CM320974I, the output of the horizontal oscillator feeds horizontal drive transistor 7408 (see **Figure 9.6**). The output of this transistor feeds the primary of horizontal drive transformer 5401. The secondary of this transformer feeds the horizontal output transistor.

In the NEC Multisync 4D, pin 13 of the horizontal oscillator feeds driver transistor Q544 (see **Figure 9.7**), a 2SK699 MOSFET. The output of this transistor feeds the primary of horizontal drive transformer T550. The secondary of this transformer drives horizontal output transistor Q560, a 2SC3688.

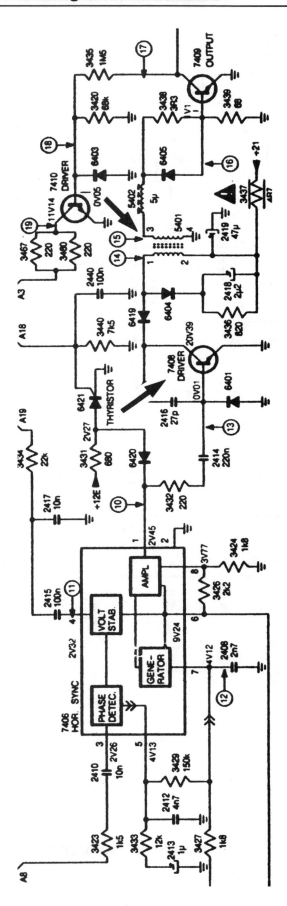

Figure 9.6. In the Magnavox 6CM3209741, the output of the horizontal oscillator feeds horizontal drive transistor 7408.

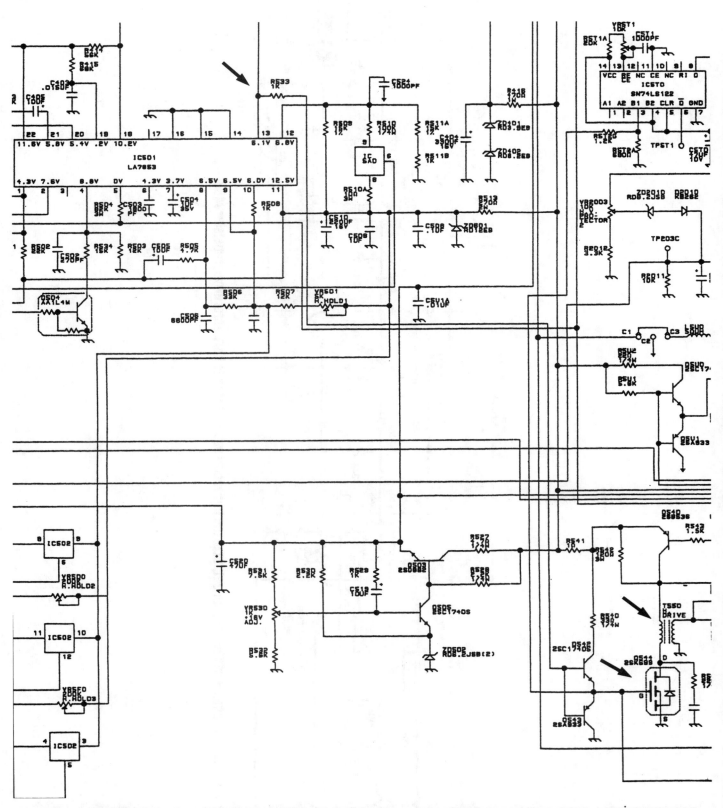

Figure 9.7. In the NEC Multisync 4D, pin 13 of the horizontal oscillator feeds driver transistor Q544, a 2SK699 MOSFET.

The Samtron SC-728SXL has two sets of horizontal drive transistors and drive transformers connected to the output of the horizontal oscillator. One transistor/transformer drive combination connects to a horizontal output transistor to produce the horizontal deflection voltage, and the other connects to another horizontal output transistor to produce the high voltage required by the anode. This is a typical design for a larger size monitor.

The output of the horizontal oscillator IC feeds two horizontal driver transistors, Q503 and Q409, which are IRF610 MOSFETs (see **Figure 9.8**). The output of Q503 feeds the primary of transformer T501, while the output of Q409 feeds the primary of T401. The secondary of T501 feeds the base of horizontal output transistor Q504, while the secondary of T401 feeds the base of Q408. Both transistors are the same type—MJW16212.

9.4 Horizontal Output Transistor

The horizontal output transistor, which we covered in the previous chapter, is covered from a different perspective here. The base of the horizontal output transistor is fed from the secondary of the horizontal drive transformer. The output of the horizontal output transistor drives the horizontal deflection yoke.

The Magnavox 6CM320974I uses a classical hookup. The base of horizontal output transistor 7409 is driven by the secondary of transformer 5401 (see **Figure 9.9**). The collector of the output transistor goes to pin 1 of the horizontal deflection yoke. Pin 1 gets voltage from the power supply. Capacitor 2431 filters any DC voltages.

Notice that from the collector of 7409 to the yoke are three damper diodes: 6409, 6408 and 6410. The first is a UF5404; the other two are MUR4100s, which work together as one diode (see **Figure 9.10**). These diodes serve different purposes. When the voltage to the horizontal deflection yoke rises, it uses one damper diode; when it collapses, it uses the other damper diode. This arrangement is called a "split" damper diode.

In the same area of the schematic are several capacitors. Capacitor 2422 is a timing capacitor. This sets the time for how long the transistor will stay on to charge the flyback transformer.

In the NEC Multisync 4D, horizontal output transistor Q560 (see **Figure 9.11**), a 2SC3688, is fed from the secondary of horizontal drive transformer T550. The output of Q560 drives the horizontal deflection yoke. Note that one page of the schematic does not show the connection to the horizontal deflection yoke, while another page indicates the connection. More information about this particular schematic is given in Chapter 16 in the section on service manuals.

Remember, in the Samtron SC-728SXL, the horizontal oscillator feeds two horizontal drive transistor/transformer combinations. These, in turn, drive two MJW16212 horizontal output transistors, Q504 and Q408. Notice in the schematic of **Figure 9.12** that Q504 is connected as an emitter follower. This is not a typical configuration for the horizontal output transistor.

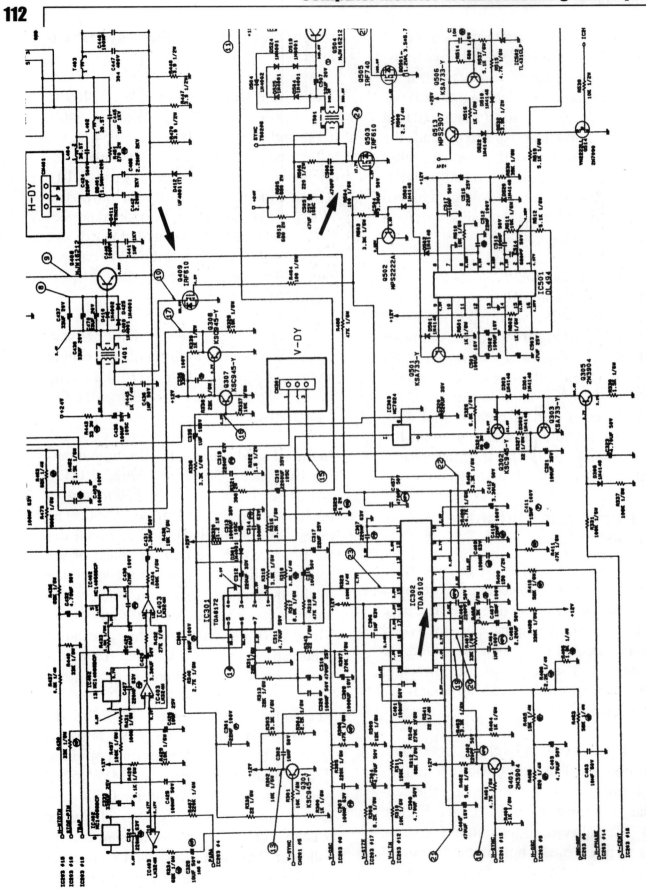

Figure 9.8. In the Samtron SC-728SXL, the output of the horizontal oscillator IC feeds two horizontal driver transistors, Q503 and Q409, which are IRF610 MOSFETs.

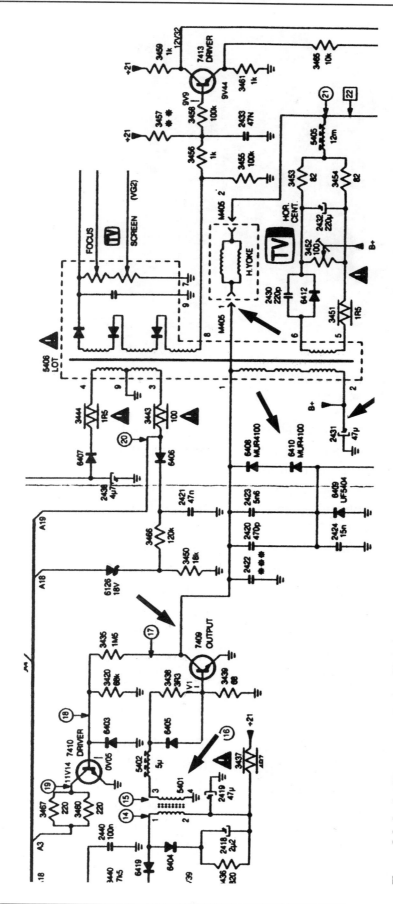

Figure 9.9. In the Magnavox 6CM3209741, the secondary of transformer 5401 drives the base of horizontal output transistor 7409. The collector of 7409 drives pin 1 of the horizontal deflection yoke.

Figure 9.10. In the Magnavox 6CM320974I, diode UF5404 and the two MUR4100s form an arrangement called a "split" damper diode.

What happens is the collector of Q504 receives power from the power supply (195 volts). The signal from horizontal drive transformer T501 goes to the base of Q504. From the base, the signal goes to the emitter, which is connected to coil T503. From here, the signal drives pin 2 of the flyback. Pin 1 of the flyback, through capacitor C511, connects back to the collector of Q504. If you measured at the collector of Q504, you would not see any waveform, only a DC voltage. The signal is at the emitter. This is a variation of the typical design.

The other horizontal output transistor, Q408, drives the horizontal deflection yoke. Pin 1 of the yoke is attached directly to the collector of the output transistor. Notice that pin 3 of the yoke is hooked up to a relay. This relay is controlled by the microprocessor and is turned on or off depending on the video mode of operation.

The picture becomes larger or smaller depending on the mode.

This monitor uses a split horizontal output for the flyback and for the yoke. In this design, one horizontal output transistor is dedicated to driving the horizontal deflection yoke. This design can thus accommodate the values needed to provide multisync operation. The NEC Multisync uses a similar split output technique, but does not feed two drive transistors from the same horizontal oscillator output.

9.5 Horizontal Controls

The horizontal controls allow you to fine tune the behavior of the electron beam as it travels from left to right in the monitor. These controls are usually found on the main PC board in the monitor, along with the rest of the horizontal circuits.

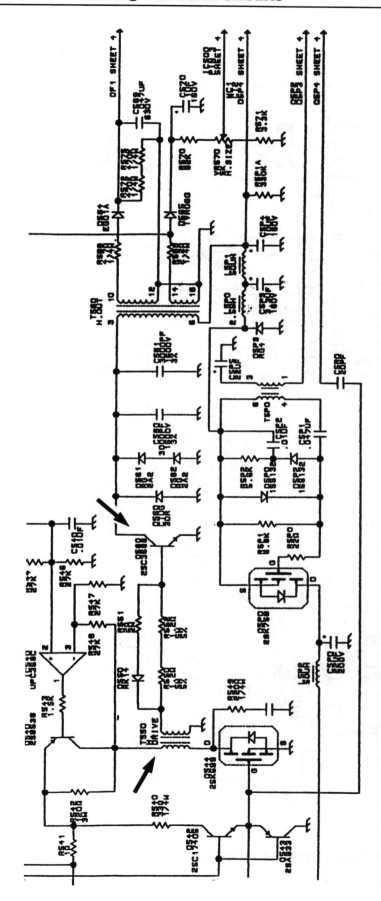

Figure 9.11. In the NEC Multisync 4D, the secondary of horizontal drive transformer T550 drives horizontal output transistor Q560, a 2SC3688. The output of Q560 drives the horizontal deflection yoke.

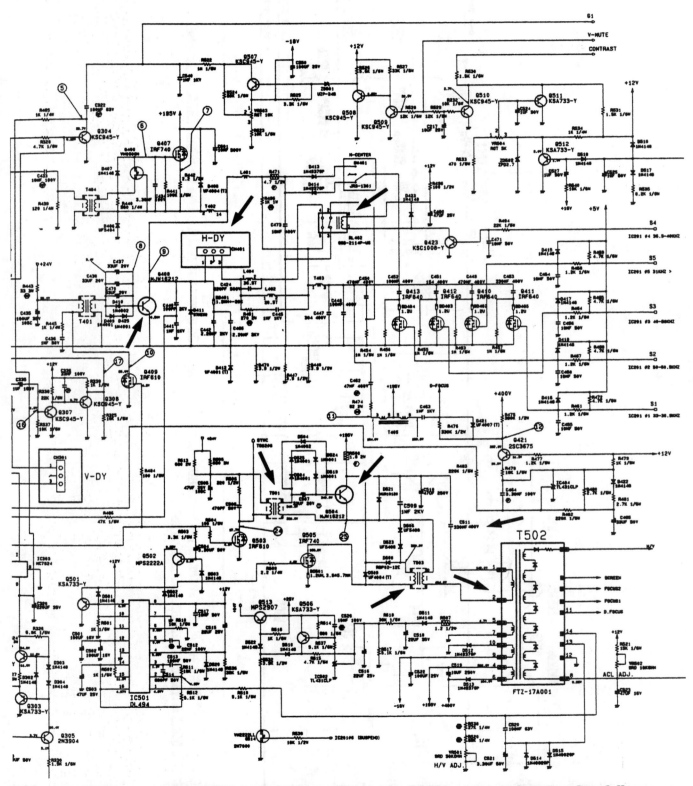

Figure 9.12. In the Samtron SC-728SXL, horizontal output transistor Q504 is connected as an emitter follower.

Horizontal Sync (Hold)

The horizontal sync control is used to stabilize the picture in the horizontal direction. Sometimes, a multiple-frequency monitor may not sync properly in one or more video modes (VGA, SVGA, etc.). This may be due to an incompatibility between the graphics adapter and the monitor. Or, the monitor may need a slight adjustment. Usually, there are horizontal sync controls on the main PC board to make this adjustment (see **Figure 9.13**). These are clearly marked for each mode in a multi-frequency monitor.

If you have a frequency counter, making this adjustment is a lot easier. You can use the frequency counter to find out what frequency is being output from the video card. Make this measurement right at pin 13 of the card's output connector. The metal shell of the connector is a good ground. A good place to make a frequency measurement in the monitor is at the output of the horizontal drive transistor. This transistor has relatively low power and voltage and will not damage the counter. If you have Sencore equipment, like the SC61 shown in **Figure 9.14**, you can go directly to the horizontal output transistor and measure the frequency. Then, you can adjust the frequency until it matches the frequency of the video card. Once you do this, the monitor will sync every time.

Horizontal Linearity

The control for horizontal linearity is a coil (see **Figure 9.15**). If the image on the screen is not evenly spaced horizontally, you can adjust this coil (by turning the core of the coil up or down). The horizontal linearity coil is connected between the horizontal output transistor and the horizontal deflection yoke. In the Magnavox 6CM320974I, the horizontal linearity coil is 5403 (see **Figure 9.16**).

When the electron beam travels from left to right to create the picture, the speed of the beam is not constant. The purpose of the coil is to equalize the speed of the beam. The result is that objects on the left side of the screen have the same horizontal length as the objects on the right. Sometimes this coil has a provision for adjustment, with a small plastic screwdriver. In other cases, there is no provision for adjustment, as it is preset at the factory.

One problem you may come across is a single vertical line down the center of the screen. Obviously, this means that there is a problem with the horizontal deflection. What causes this? Sometimes, after years of using the monitor, solder joints of the horizontal linearity coil may crack or break due to temperature differences. When this happens, it is as if the horizontal yoke is disconnected from the printed circuit board. There is no horizontal deflection, but there is still the vertical deflection. So, you get a line in the middle of the screen from top to bottom.

Horizontal Shift (Position or Phase)

The horizontal shift control slightly changes the phase of the angle. This moves the image on the screen to the right or left of center. The picture has the same linearity, the same size, everything is the same, but it moves sideways on the screen. In the Magnavox 6CM320974I, this control

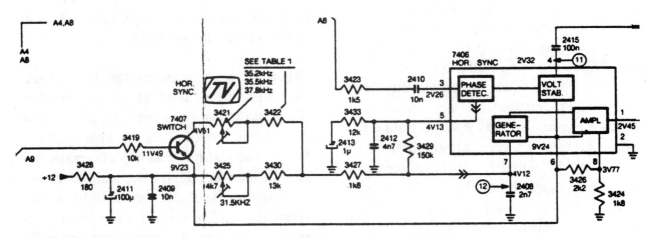

Figure 9.13. The horizontal sync control in the Magnavox 6CM320974I monitor.

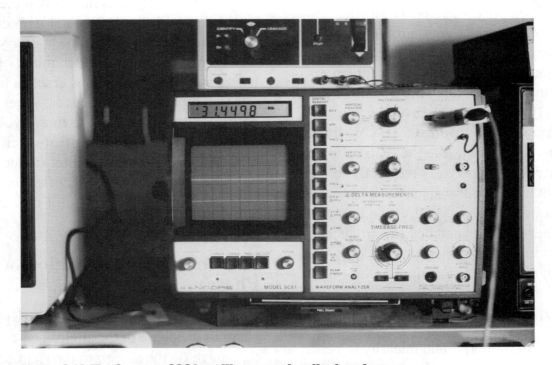

Figure 9.14. The Sencore SC61 oscilloscope also displays frequency.

Figure 9.15. The horizontal linearity coil in the Magnavox 6CM320974I.

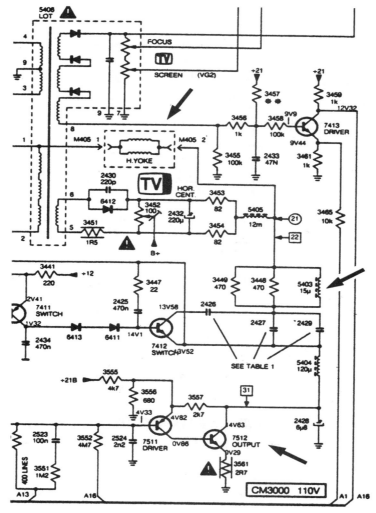

Figure 9.16. In the Magnavox 6CM320974I, the horizontal linearity coil is 5403.

is 3413 and 3414 depending on the frequency (see **Figure 9.17**).

Horizontal Center

The horizontal center control actually moves the raster, not the image, from side to side. This lets you adjust the exact geometrical center of the picture tube. If for any reason the horizontal deflection is cut off, you will see a line running from top to bottom on the display. This line should be exactly at the geometrical center of the picture tube. This adjustment is made with a heavy duty control, normally about 100 to

150 ohms. In the Magnavox 6CM320974I, this is component 3452 (see **Figure 9.18**). The control is typically a wire-wound potentiometer. You can see it to the left of the horizontal linearity control in **Figure 9.15**). This control is not affected by the different modes of operation.

Horizontal Width (Size)

The horizontal width control is an active circuit in a computer monitor. For some applications, you need to adjust the size of the screen horizontally. This is the purpose of the horizontal width circuit. A typical

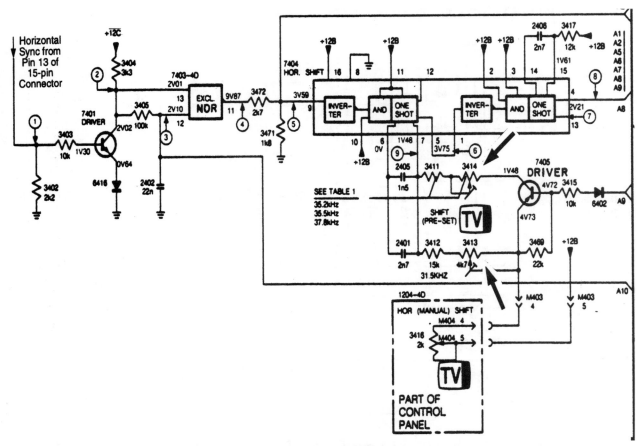

Figure 9.17. The horizontal shift control in the Magnavox 6CM320974I is 3413 and 3414, depending on the frequency.

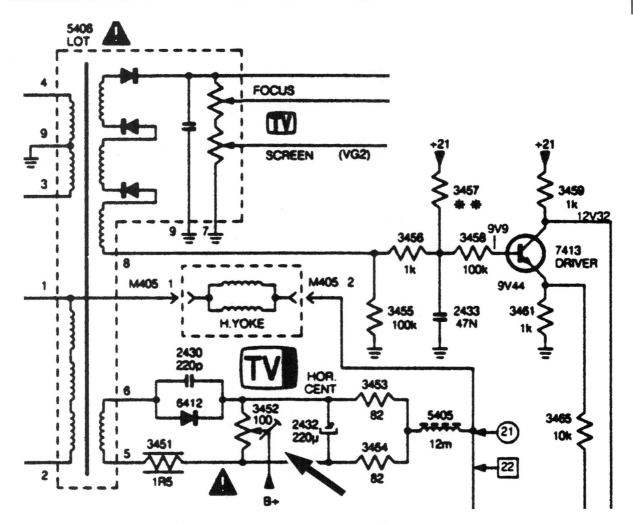

Figure 9.18. The horizontal center control in the Magnavox 6CM320974I is component 3452. This control is typically a wire-wound potentiometer.

circuit, such as the one in the Magnavox 6CM320974I (see **Figure 9.19**), consists of two or three transistors and a control on the front or the side of the monitor to adjust the horizontal width. **Figure 9.20** shows how transistors 7412 and 7512 are positioned on the main board of the

Magnavox. An active circuit such as this one can have problems such as a bad transistor, a bad solder joint, or a burned resistor. A complete description of this type of problem can be found in case study 2 of Appendix B.

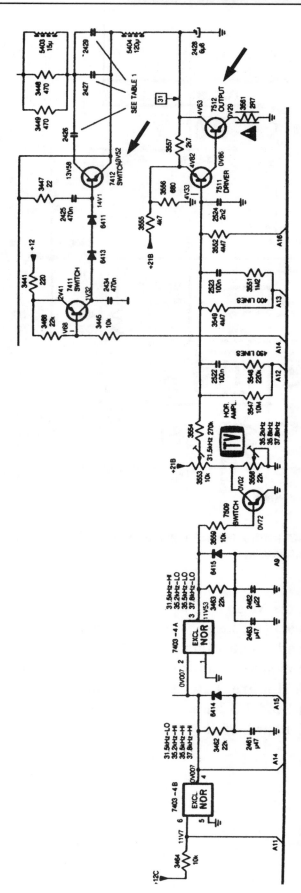

Figure 9.19. The horizontal width control in the Magnavox 6CM320974I monitor.

Figure 9.20. Transistors 7412 and 7512 on the main board of the Magnavox monitor.

Chapter 10

Troubleshooting Vertical Circuits

The vertical circuits are responsible for driving the vertical deflection yoke on the neck of the CRT. This causes the electron beam to move from the top of the screen to the bottom and back up again to create the picture. The vertical circuits consist of the vertical oscillator and vertical output circuits, as well as the vertical controls for sync, phase, linearity, position and height. These circuits typically reside on the main PC board in a computer monitor (see **Figure 10.1**).

10.1 The Vertical Circuits

The vertical oscillator may run at the rate of 56 Hz, 60 Hz, 72 Hz or other value depending on the video mode selected by the user. If it is running at 60 Hz, then the picture on the screen changes 60 times every second.

The vertical oscillator actually delivers a sawtooth shaped signal (see **Figure 10.2**). This signal is supposed to drive the vertical deflection yoke. But, the signal that comes from the oscillator is not strong enough to do this, so it goes to a vertical output circuit, which amplifies the signal.

In order to do its job, the vertical oscillator has to be synchronized with the signal that is coming from the computer. The computer sends the vertical sync pulse on pin 14 of the 15-pin video connector. The vertical sync triggers the oscillator (and thus the electron beam) to start working at the beginning of the frame. In other words, the beam starts from the top of the screen. The end of the sync is normally the bottom of the screen. This way the beam gets deflected vertically from top to bottom.

Figure 10.1. The vertical circuits on the main PC board of the NEC Multisync 4D; the vertical circuits IC is attached to a heat sink.

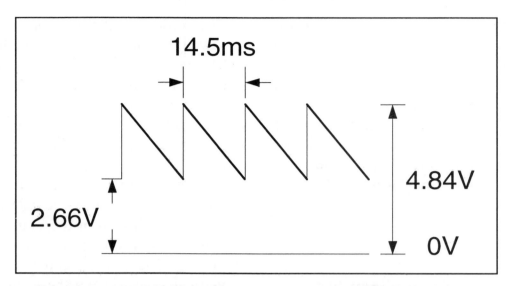

Figure 10.2. The vertical oscillator delivers a sawtooth shaped signal.

In the Magnavox 6CM320974I monitor, the vertical oscillator and the vertical output are together in one integrated circuit. The vertical sync signal at pin 14 of the video connector goes through a series of amplifications (see **Figure 10.3**). The output amplifier is 7501, an emitter follower. From the emitter of this transistor, the signal goes to pin 5 of vertical IC 7502. As shown in the block diagram of the IC (see **Figure 10.4**), this IC has a generator, which is synchronized by the vertical sync signal, depending on the video mode. This IC also has a voltage stabilizer. In other words, it has a voltage regulator. This stabilizer is getting +21 volts from the power supply, and it feeds voltages to the various circuits inside the IC.

From this point, the generated signal is synchronized and goes to a sawtooth generator, which changes the shape of the signal to a sawtooth shape. From there the signal goes to an operational amplifier, which is a high-gain amplifier. The signal is then fed to the output amplifier. This amplifier also contains protection circuitry.

This protects against overheating, overloading, and so forth. The amplified signal leaves the IC at pin 1 and goes to pin 3 of the vertical deflection yoke (also known as a frame deflection yoke). The signal exits the yoke at pin 4.

Pin 4 of the yoke has to be somehow connected to ground. Typically, the circuitry consists of a large electrolytic capacitor and a small resistor. In this case, the capacitor is 2514, which has a value of 4,700 microfarads, and the resistor is 3519, which has a value of 2 ohms (see **Figure 10.5**). This closes the loop. To sum up, the signal leaves from the output at pin 1 of the vertical IC, goes to the yoke, the capacitor, the resistor, and then to ground. The vertical deflection yoke is the load of the integrated circuit.

In the NEC Multisync 4D, the vertical circuits are contained in IC432, generic part number LA7838 (see **Figure 10.6**). The IC is powered at pin 1 (12 volts) and pin 8 (24 volts). The vertical sync signal enters the IC at pin 2. The vertical oscillator,

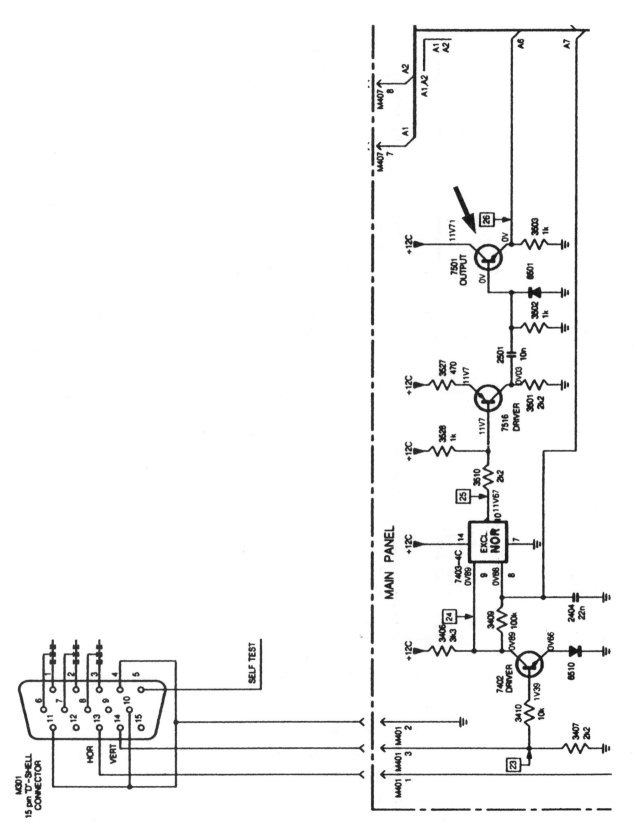

Figure 10.3. In the Magnavox 6CM320974I monitor, the vertical sync signal at pin 14 of the video connector goes through a series of amplifications; the output amplifier is 7501.

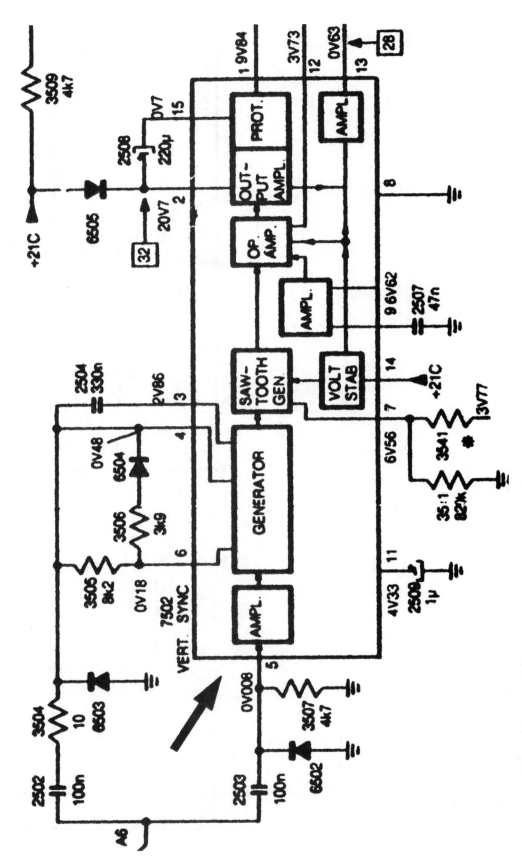

Figure 10.4. In the Magnavox 6CM320974I monitor, vertical IC 7502 has a generator, which is synchronized by the vertical sync signal.

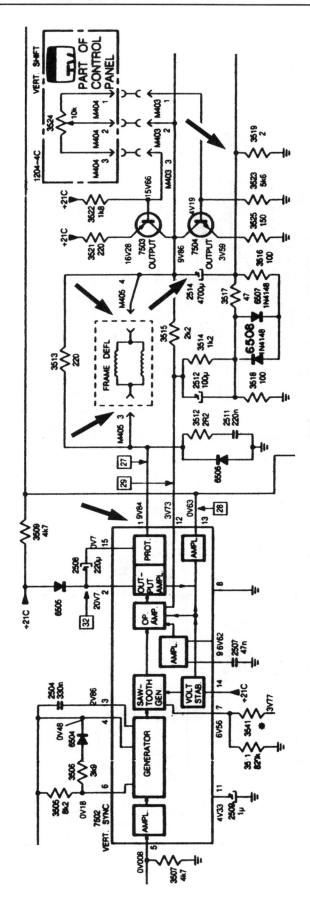

Figure 10.5. In the Magnavox 6CM320974I monitor, pin 4 of the yoke is connected to ground through capacitor is 2514 and resistor 3519.

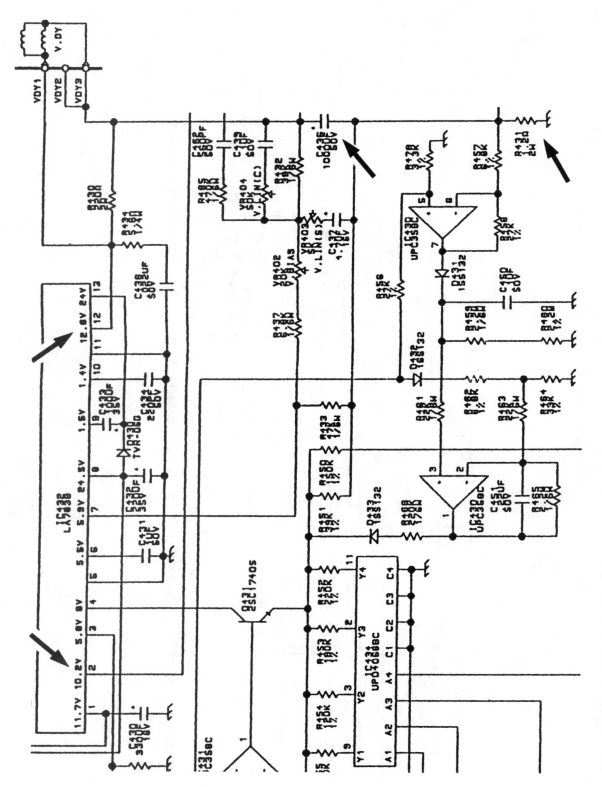

Figure 10.6. In the NEC Multisync 4D, the vertical circuits are contained in IC432.

sawtooth generator and vertical output are built into the IC. The output is at pin 12, which goes to pin 1 of the vertical deflection yoke. The other side of the yoke, pin 3, goes to the positive lead of electrolytic capacitor C436, which has a value of 1,000 microfarads rated at 50 volts. The negative side of this capacitor goes to ground through resistor R431, which has a value of 1.2 ohms rated at 2 watts. So, the loop is closed. To sum up, the signal generated in IC432 leaves at pin 12, goes to the vertical deflection coil, then to capacitor C436, to resistor R431, and then to ground.

In these two monitors all the vertical circuits—vertical oscillator, sawtooth generator, operational amplifier, and vertical out-put—are all built into a single IC. Everything is there. This is in sharp contrast to the horizontal circuits in these monitors. Though this is the case in the Magnavox and NEC monitors, this is not the case in the Samtron monitor.

The setup of the vertical circuits in the Samtron SC-728SXL monitor is somewhat different. This monitor has a separate vertical output integrated circuit, IC301 (see **Figure 10.7**). The generic part number of this power amplifier IC is TDA8172. The output of this circuit drives the yoke. In order for it to do this, it has to get the signal from the vertical oscillator.

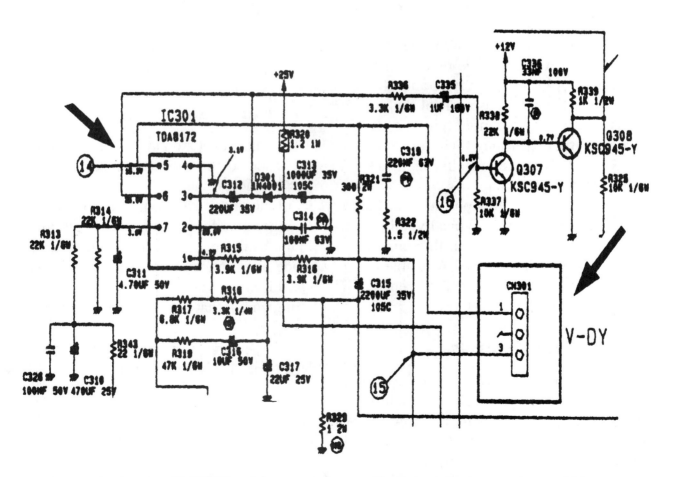

Figure 10.7. The Samtron SC-728SXL employs a separate vertical output integrated circuit, IC301.

The vertical oscillator in this monitor, IC302 (generic part number TDA9102), is combined together on the same IC as the horizontal oscillator (see **Figure 10.8**). The vertical sync signal from pin 14 of the 15-pin connector enters IC302 on pin 14. The output of this IC is pin 15.

The output of IC302 feeds pin 1 of IC301, the input of the power amplifier, through resistor R317. The amplified output of IC301 exits at pin 5. This signal drives the vertical deflection yoke at pin 1 of the yoke. The signal exits the yoke at pin 3 and goes through resistor R324, which has a value of 68 ohms rated at 3 watts. Then it goes through capacitor C321, which has a value of 100 microfarads rated at 35 volts (see **Figure 10.9**). So, the loop is closed.

Notice, in the Samtron monitor the resistor and capacitor are in the reverse order compared with the Magnavox and NEC monitors. This is because part of the output is sent back to the input (pin 1) of the vertical output IC through resistors R316 and R315. This creates negative feedback.

The output IC also gets power from the power supply on pin 2. Typically, this IC gets 35 volts at this pin. In this circuit, though, the IC gets 25 volts. A fusible resistor, R230, is connected between the power supply and pin 2.

10.2 Vertical Controls

The vertical controls allow you to fine tune the behavior of the electron beam as it travels from top to bottom in the monitor. These controls are usually found on the main PC board in the monitor, along with the rest of the vertical circuits.

Vertical Linearity

The vertical linearity control allows you to make the top and the bottom of the picture evenly spaced. In the NEC, the vertical linearity control, VR403, is connected to pin 7 of IC432 (see **Figure 10.10**). A problem with this control means there is a problem with either the potentiometer or the IC.

Vertical Shift (Position or Phase)

This control is used to shift the image up and down on the raster. In other words, this control lets you move the picture up and down, but the raster stays the same. In the Magnavox monitor, the vertical shift control is a 10 kilohm potentiometer, 3524. This pot is connected to the operational amplifier in vertical sync chip 7502 through pin 12 (see **Figure 10.11**)

Vertical Center

The vertical center control actually moves the raster, not the image, up and down. This lets you adjust the exact geometrical center of the raster. This control is not present in either the Magnavox or NEC monitors. In the Samtron monitor, this adjustment is made automatically by the microprocessor. **Figure 10.12** shows the vertical centering circuit that the microprocessor controls.

Vertical Height (Size)

The vertical height control allows you to adjust the size of the picture from top to bottom. In the Magnavox, there are actually four vertical size controls, one for each video mode supported by the monitor.

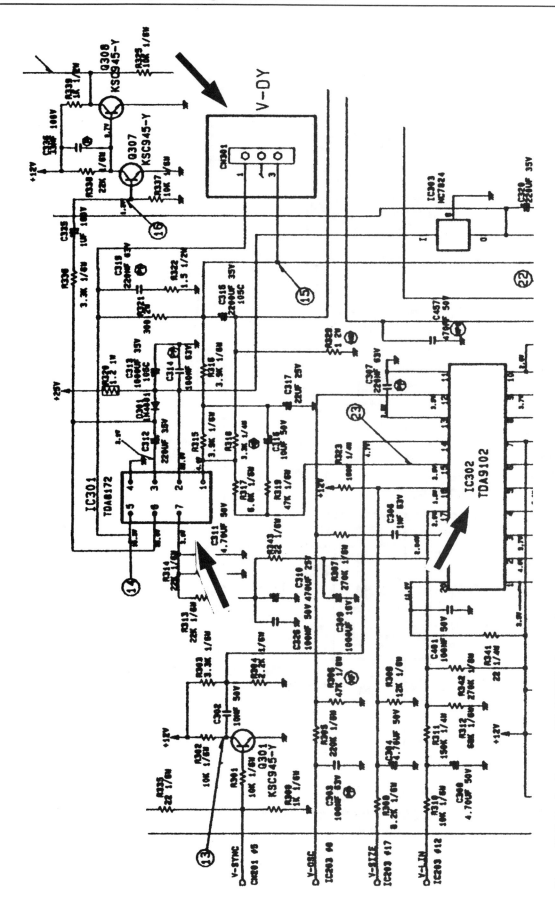

Figure 10.8. In the Samtron SC-728SXL, the vertical oscillator is on the same IC (IC302) as the horizontal oscillator. The poor quality of the figure is due to the fact that it has been enlarged ten times its normal size.

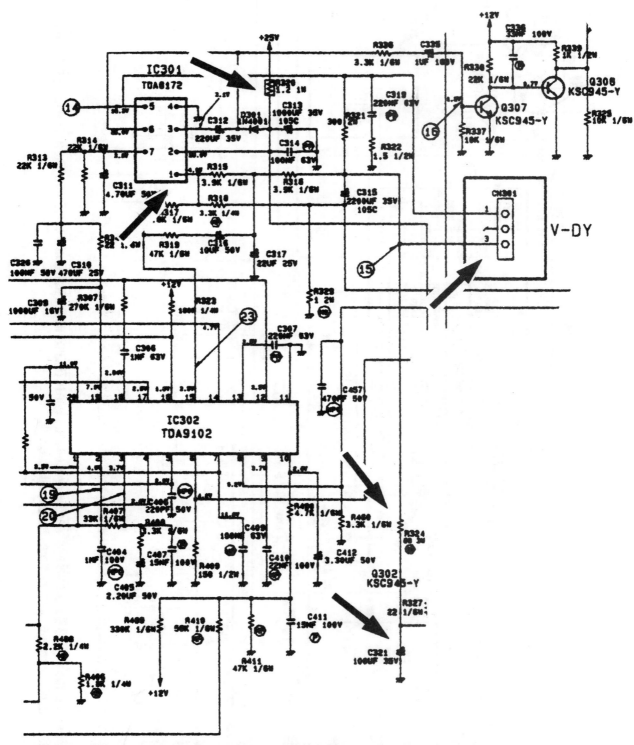

Figure 10.9. In the Samtron SC-728SXL, the vertical signal exits the yoke at pin 3 and goes through resistor R324 and capacitor C321 to ground.

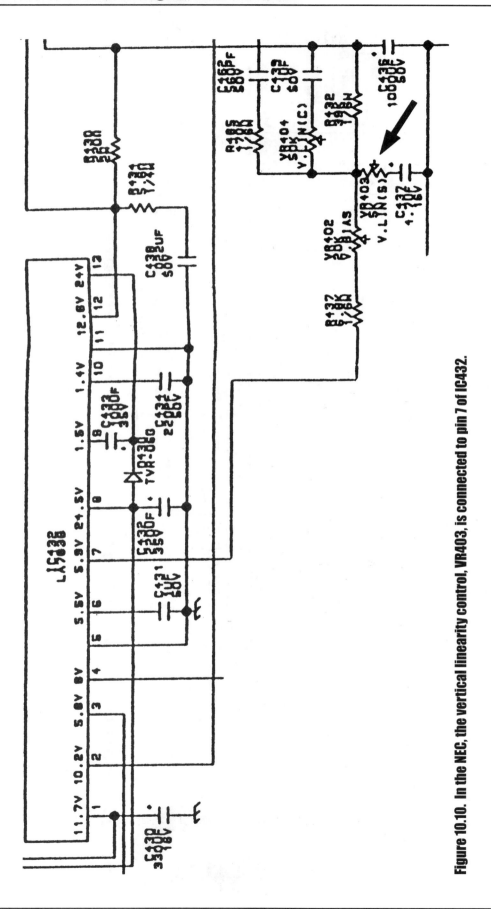

Figure 10.10. In the NEC, the vertical linearity control, VR403, is connected to pin 7 of IC432.

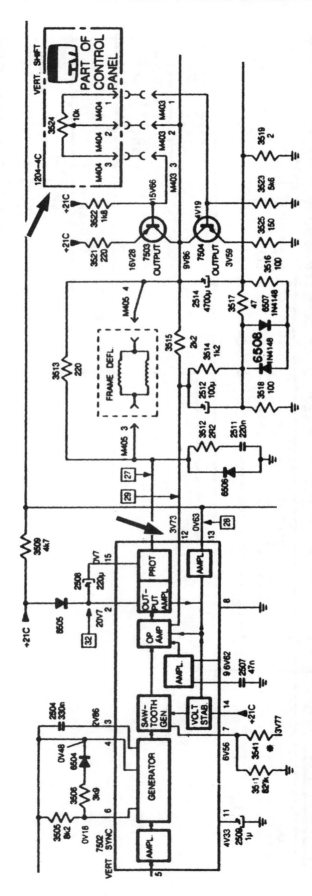

Figure 10.11. In the Magnavox monitor, the vertical shift control is 3524. This pot is connected to the operational amplifier in vertical sync chip 7502 through pin 12.

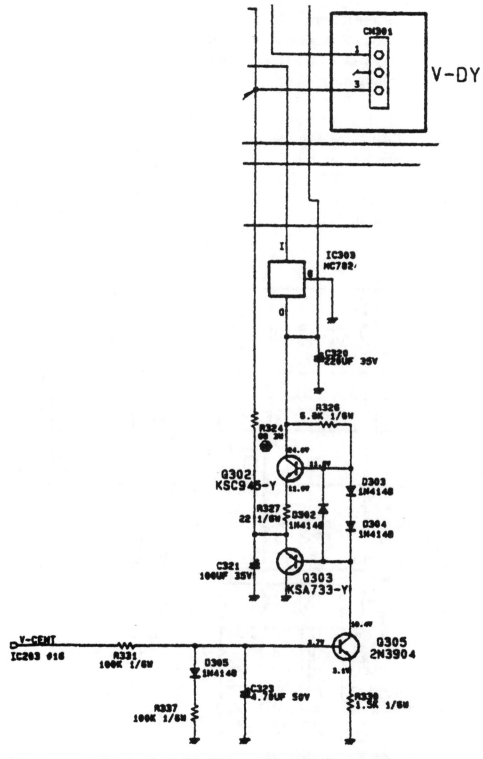

Figure 10.12. In the Samtron monitor, the microprocessor controls the vertical centering circuit.

These are potentiometers 3536 through 3539 (see **Figure 10.13**). Logic switch 7508 selects the mode of operation. Adjusting the corresponding control varies the input to pin 7 of the vertical sync IC, 7502, which varies the vertical height.

In the NEC, the vertical height is controlled by a small trimpot, DR405 (see **Figure 10.14**). This trimpot varies one input to IC431, which drives transistor Q431. The output of Q431 connects to pin 4 of IC432. Thus, turning the trimpot controls the vertical size function of the IC.

IC434 does the video mode switching for the vertical circuits of IC432. IC434 is controlled by the CPU. Depending on the video mode, IC434 activates one of four outputs. This active output connects to one input of IC431 and also to the emitter of transistor Q431.

10.3 Troubleshooting Vertical Circuits

You may want to check the vertical IC for correct operation if you suspect that the vertical oscillator is not working. You will

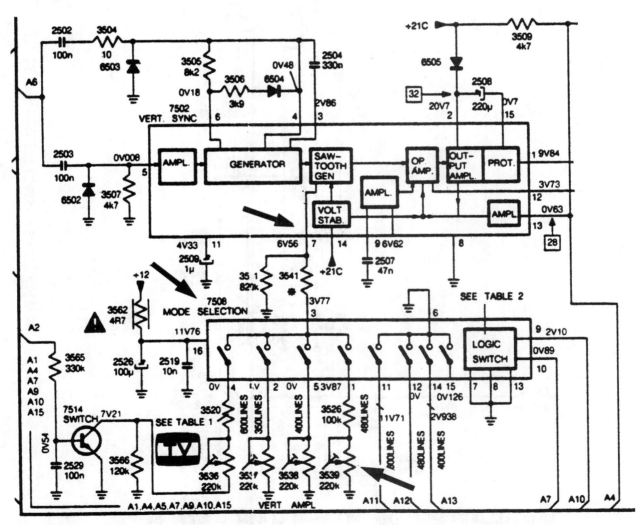

Figure 10.13. In the Magnavox, there are four vertical size controls, one for each video mode supported by the monitor. These are potentiometers 3536 through 3539; logic switch 7508 selects the mode of operation.

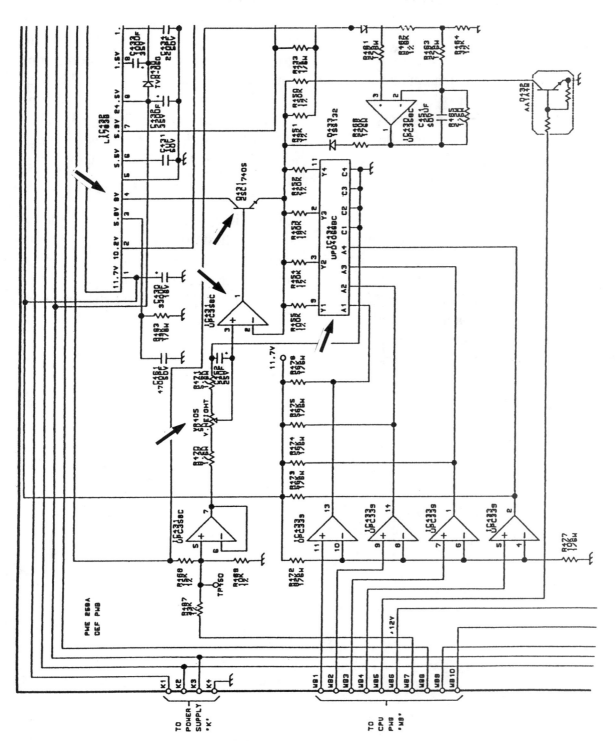

Figure 10.14. In the NEC, the vertical height is controlled by a small trimpot, VR405.

need the service manual and a DMM to do this. It's also a good idea to use an oscilloscope to check the waveform at the output of the vertical IC.

By checking the voltages at the various pins of the vertical IC, you can get an idea if the chip is getting power or if the vertical oscillator is producing any signal. If the IC is not getting power, then you should check the power supply circuits or some related component that is cutting the power to the vertical oscillator.

A very common failure in the vertical circuit is not the oscillator itself, but output circuit. The output circuit is one of the most stressed parts in the monitor. Normally, when the monitor runs for a long period of time, several hours or more, the vertical output IC becomes very hot. High tempera-

tures create problems after years of use. A typical problem is a cracked solder joint, which loosens up the connection between the printed circuit board and the IC. Also, the high temperature may destroy the integrated circuit altogether by shorting some of the components inside of it. If this happens, all you will see is a horizontal line across the middle of the display. This is a failure of the output circuit even though the oscillator may still be producing a signal.

If the vertical output IC shorts out, the resistor and diode that go to the secondary winding of the high-voltage transformer may be destroyed. If this happens, replacing only the IC will not fix the problem. So, remember to check all related components.

Chapter 11

Troubleshooting Video Circuits

In a computer monitor, the video signal contains the information used to develop the picture you see on the display. The video signal is created inside the computer and sent to the monitor as separate red, green and blue signals on pins 1, 2, and 3, respectively, of the 15-pin video connector. The monitor's job is to amplify this signal so that it can drive the red, blue and green "guns" of the cathode ray tube.

In this chapter, we show you how the video signal progresses from input to output in the NEC Multisync 4D. These circuits are on a separate printed circuit board at the rear of the monitor. The behavior of the video circuits in the NEC Mulitsync 4D is typical of the process that occurs in most VGA/SVGA-type computer monitors.

11.1 The Video Circuits

The video signal enters the video board at pins 1 (red), 2 (green), and 3 (blue) of the 15-pin video connector (see **Figure 11.1**). In the case of the NEC 4D, this connector is at the rear of the monitor (see **Figure 11.2**). In other monitors, the connector may be found at the end of a video signal cable.

In the NEC, each of the video signals goes to a small coil (LC705/6/7). This coil looks like a blue capacitor, but has three pins. The middle pin of this coil goes to ground, while the other two are the input and output. From here, the signal goes to a coupling capacitor (C204/5/6), which blocks any DC portion of the signal but allows the AC to pass through.

Next, each of the video signals goes to the base of a transistor (Q704/5/6). These transistors are so-called emitter followers.

Figure 11.2. In the NEC Multisync 4D, the 15-pin connector is at the rear of the monitor.

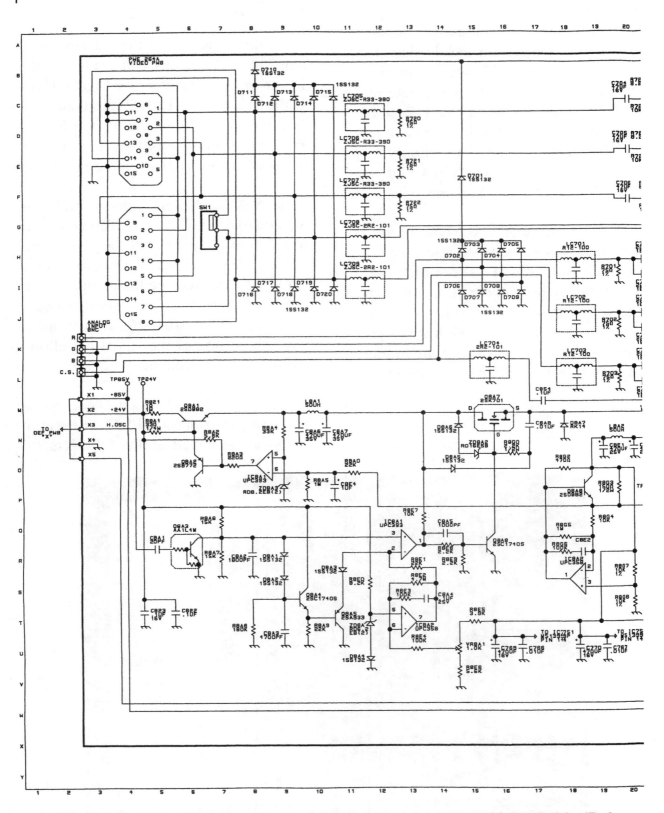

Figure 11.1. The video signal enters the video board at pins 1 (red), 2 (green), and 3 (blue) of the 15-pin video connector.

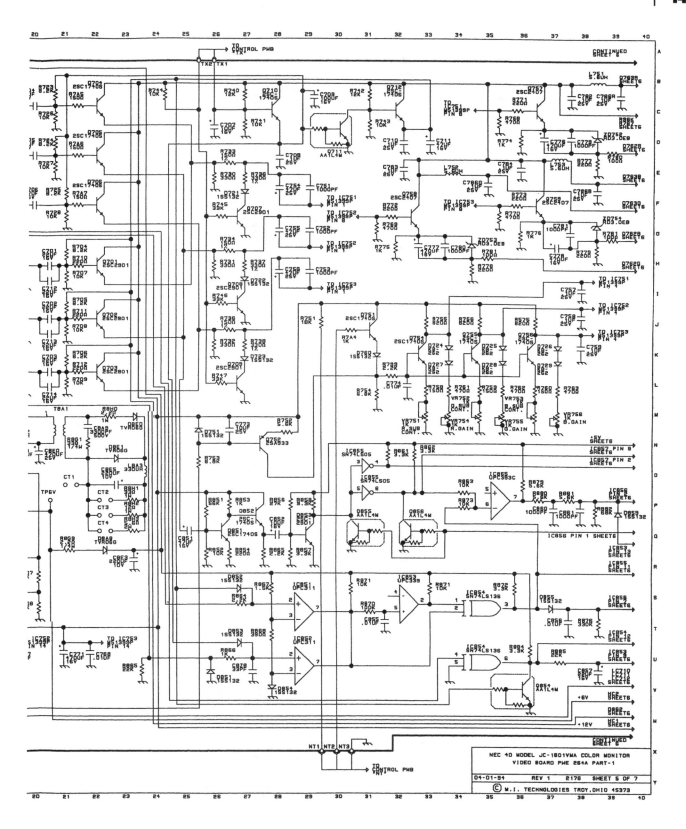

NEC 4D MODEL JC-1601VMA COLOR MONITOR
VIDEO BOARD PWE 264A PART-1

04-01-94 | REV 1 | 2176 | SHEET 5 OF 7

© M.I. TECHNOLOGIES TROY,OHIO 45373

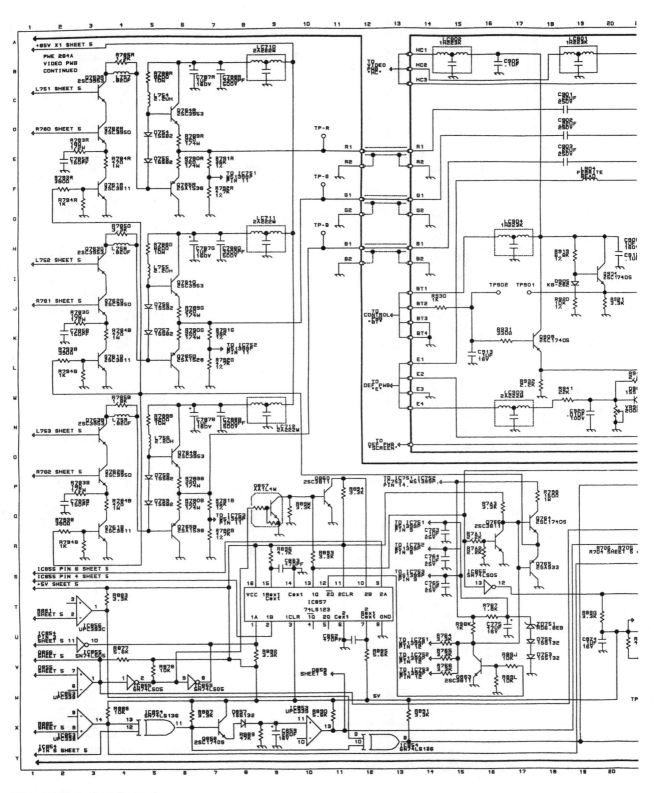

Figure 11-1. Continued.

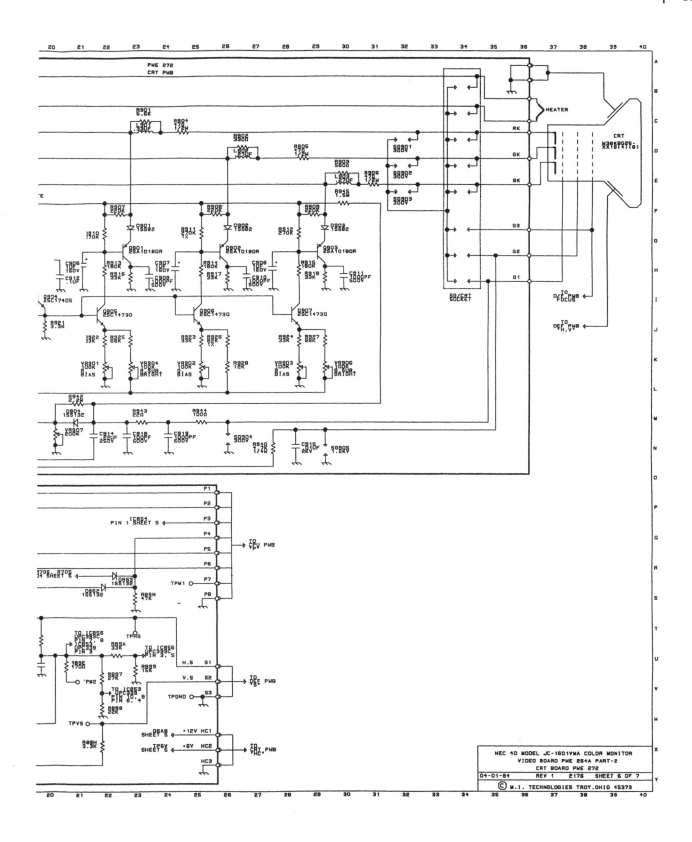

They do not amplify the signal; instead, they serve as a buffer, which has a high-impedance input and a low-impedance output. The video signal comes in at the base of the transistor and exits at the emitter at about the same voltage level.

From the emitter, the signal goes through a resistor (R733/34/36) and then to IC 751/2/3. Notice, this IC is not shown on the schematic diagram. Instead, arrows indicate that the signal goes to the input of this IC. This is not usually the case with schematic diagrams. Most times, the schematic will show the IC. But, as noted in Chapter 16, service manuals and schematic diagrams differ from manufacturer to manufacturer. You have to be able to read the schematic diagram, no matter which way it is presented to you. These three ICs can be seen on the video board of the NEC monitor. The magnitude of the video signal at the input (pin 1) of each IC (see **Figure 11.3a** and **Figure 11.3b**) is 0.7 volts. At each output (pin 8), the signal is about 2 volts higher (see **Figure 11.4a** and **Figure 11.4b**). So, each IC amplifies its part (color) of the video signal.

Next, the video signal goes through another emitter follower, Q757/8/9. From the emitter of each transistor, the video signal is fed to the base of transistor Q762R/G/B. Each of these transistors amplifies the video signal to a level of approximately 6 volts (see **Figure 11.5**). From this point, the signal is amplified again by a complementary pair of output power transistors Q764R/G/B and Q765R/G/B. This combination of NPN and PNP transistors is called a push-pull output; each color has this pair.

A push-pull amplifier has very low output impedance. It easily feeds the picture tube cathode without any distortion of the signal. We measured at the test point G (green video) and found the video signal at a level of approximately 50 volts AC (see **Figure 11.6a** and **Figure 11.6b**). This signal goes directly to the green cathode of the picture tube through a coupling capacitor C902. The red and blue signals are processed in a similar way.

11.2 Checking the Video Circuits

As mentioned, in the NEC 4D and most other computer monitors, the video circuits are on a separate video board. The signals on this video board are connected through wires to a printed circuit board that connects to the neck of the CRT. If one of these wires breaks or is disconnected, one of the colors will be missing on the monitor's display. This is very easy to notice, especially if you display a color bar pattern on the monitor.

If you notice a color missing, like blue, check the wires that connect the video board to the CRT board. A connection may be broken or a solder joint cracked. How does this happen? When you are servicing a monitor, you might turn it all around, remove the CRT board from the CRT, and so forth. With all this handling, you can easily break a connection. This may happen when you are repairing an entirely different problem. You think you have repaired the monitor, and then you find out you have another problem—a color is missing. So, look for wires that may have pulled loose from their connections. If

Figure 11.3a. In the NEC Multisync 4D, measuring the magnitude of the video signal at the input (pin 1) of IC752.

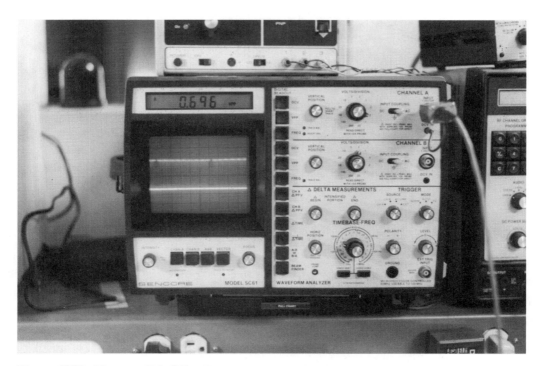

Figure 11.3b. The result is 0.7 volts.

Figure 11.4a. In the NEC Multisync 4D, measuring the magnitude of the video signal at the output (pin 8) of IC752.

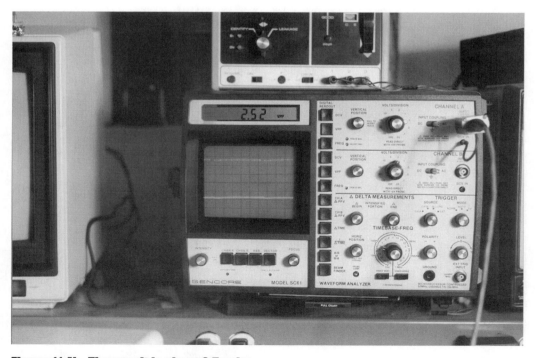

Figure 11.4b. The result is about 2.5 volts.

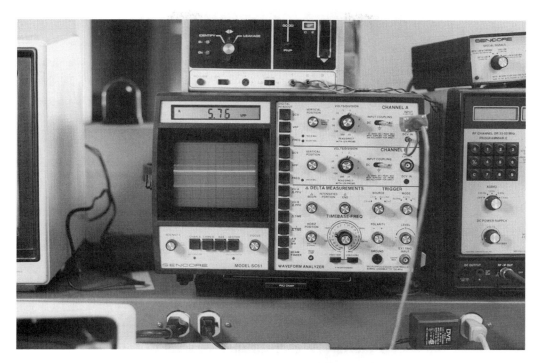

Figure 11.5. The magnitude of the video signal amplified by transistor Q762R/G/B is approximately 6 volts.

Figure 11.6a. Measuring at the test point G (green video).

Figure 11.6b. The video signal level is approximately 50 volts AC.

there are no loose wires, look for cracked solder joints.

If all connections appear to be okay, make measurements at the video output transistors. First, measure the DC voltages at all three transistors. These voltages should be almost equal (a small discrepancy is okay). These transistor amplifiers are highly stressed components. Solder joints may crack from the heat, the transistors may short, or a resistor connected to the transistor may overheat and blow open. .

The location of the video output transistors varies from monitor to monitor. In the Magnavox 6CM320974I monitor, the CRT board that connects the socket of the picture tube to the rest of the monitor has no transistors. All the active circuitry is located on a printed circuit board surrounding the CRT board (see **Figure 11.7**). The

power transistors are on this video board (see **Figure 11.8**).

In the NEC Multisync 4D, the CRT board contains the CRT socket and a few transistors. The video board is a large printed circuit just inside the back cover connected to one of the monitor's metal shields. This board contains all the video circuitry.

Keep in mind that the video signals are generated inside the computer, not inside the monitor. The computer monitor contains only amplification circuits for each color. That's all these circuits do.

11.3 The Signal Cable

The signal cable has a 15-pin D-type connector at one end, which connects to the 15-pin video connector at the computer. Once inside the computer monitor, the signal cable is split into two pieces. One is a

Figure 11.7. The video board in the Magnavox 6CM320974I monitor surrounds the CRT board.

Figure 11.8. The video output power transistors in the Magnavox 6CM320974I monitor.

7-pin plug that carries all the color video lines, with their shields. This plug usually connects to the video PC board in the computer monitor. The other is a 3-pin connector that carries the horizontal sync, vertical sync and ground. This connector usually plugs into the main printed circuit board.

If you have problem with any color, say the red color is missing on the monitor, it may be the fault of the cable. It is very easy to check if there is continuity on the cable. First, set the DMM to ohms. Then, place one lead of the DMM on the pin (of the 15-pin connector) you wish to check. The other lead should be placed at the appropriate pin on the terminating plug inside the monitor. If you are checking the red video line for continuity, for example, clip one lead of the DMM to pin 1 of the video connector. Then, place the other lead at

whichever pin of the 7-pin plug brings the red video signal to the video board. If the reading is zero ohms, the cable is okay; if not, the cable needs to be replaced.

The different colors are often silk-screened right on the video board to facilitate measurement. Or else, you can check with the service manual. Another way is to just do the measurement by trial and error. Before making any continuity measurements, unplug the monitor so that no power goes to the monitor.

In the NEC, not only is there a PC standard 15-pin video input, there is also a Macintosh standard 15-pin input, plus BNC inputs (R, G, B, and sync). If you want to check the monitor through the BNC inputs, you will need a special cable (see **Figure 11.9**). This is special cable that costs between $30 and $70. We purchased

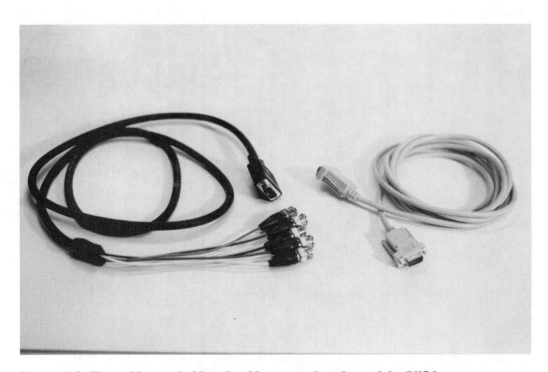

Figure 11.9. The cable needed for checking a monitor through its BNC inputs.

it for $30 from RNJ Supplies (1-800-645-5833; P/N S-H15M5BNC-6); but, we also saw a cable of this type for sale at a large computer retailer for about $70.

You should have a cable like this as part of your test equipment. If a customer wants you to check the BNC inputs of a monitor, you will need this cable to provide the signal to the monitor (see **Figure 11.10**). Another way to check a BNC input is with a high-quality piece of test equipment such as the Sencore VA62A. This video analyzer has a video output that you can apply to a monitor via a BNC cable. The VA62A has only one of these outputs, so you would have to check each monitor input separately.

11.4 Checking On-Screen Display (OSD) Circuits

Some monitors present you with an on-screen display when you press one of the control buttons. One or more ICs generate the video necessary to create the display. Of the three monitors we are covering in this book, only the Samtron has this feature.

Figure 11.11 shows the OSD circuitry in block diagram form, while **Figure 11.12** shows the schematic diagram. If a monitor with OSD fails to provide a display, you should first check that the ICs are receiving power. The OSD ICs are turned on by the microprocessor. If the OSD ICs are not turning on, you need to check if this signal is being sent by the microprocessor. You can do this with a DMM or logic probe. If the OSD ICs are powered and receiving the turn-on signal, yet still not providing an output, this is a strong indication that the ICs are defective.

Figure 11.10. Testing a monitor through its BNC inputs.

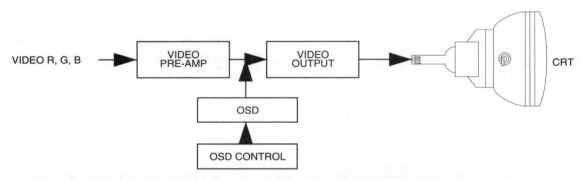

Figure 11.11 The OSD circuitry of the Samtron SC-728SXL in block diagram form.

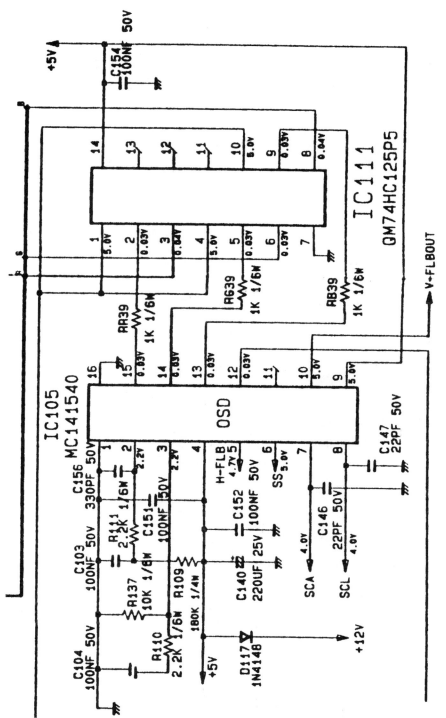

Figure 11.12. The schematic diagram of the OSD circuitry in the Samtron SC-728SXL.

Chapter 12

Troubleshooting the CRT

The cathode ray tube is a fairly reliable component in today's computer monitors. But just like anything else, it has its own share of troubles. In terms of servicing, it is very rare that you would want to replace a CRT, since the cost of this piece often rivals the cost of the entire monitor. But there are certain procedures you can perform to correct problems with the CRT.

12.1 Overview of a CRT

The CRT is a large vacuum tube with an electronic gun or cathode that emits electrons when heated by a filament (see **Figure 12.1**). The electrons travel through the tube and eventually hit a phosphorescent material on the face of the tube to produce light.

A color CRT has three guns, one for each color—red, green and blue. The guns do not emit different colors, but rather are aimed at red, green and blue phosphor elements on the face of the picture tube.

A series of grids inside the tube are used to manipulate the electron beam. In a typical monitor, such as those we are covering in this book, the first grid of the CRT (G1) controls the brightness of the display you see on the screen. The second grid (G2) accelerates the electrons. The third grid (G3) focuses the electrons. The anode delivers high voltage from the high-voltage transformer to the picture tube. **Figure 12.2** shows the schematic diagram of a typical CRT.

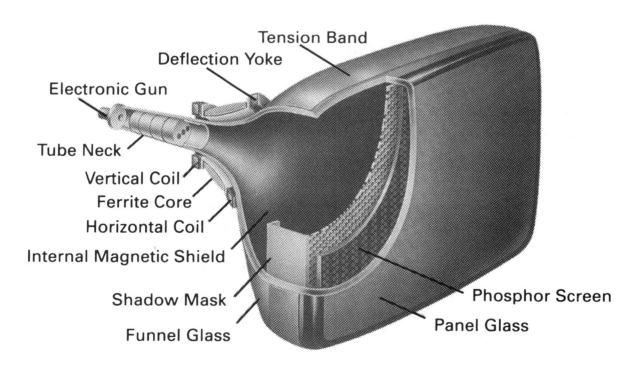

Figure 12.1. The CRT is a large vacuum tube with an electronic gun or cathode that emits electrons when heated by a filament.

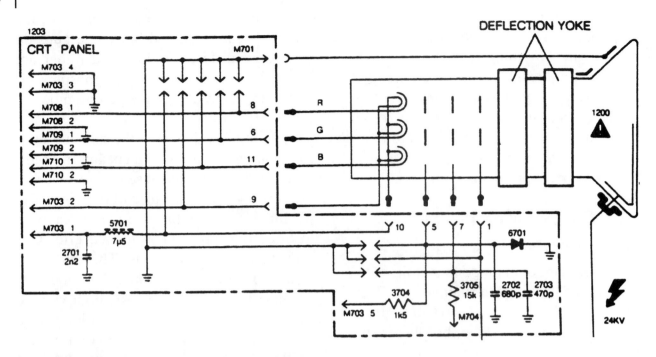

Figure 12.2. The schematic diagram of a typical CRT.

As electrons travel from the cathode to the phosphorescent face of the CRT, they pass through a shadow mask or an aperture grille (see **Figure 12.3a** and **Figure 12.3b**). These devices are designed to isolate individual picture elements or pixels, which form the image displayed on a computer's monitor. Shadow mask technology relies on an opaque sheet with small pinholes to separate pixels both horizontally and vertically. Aperture grille technology employs a series of thin, closely-spaced vertical wires to isolate pixels horizontally. The pixels are separated vertically by the nature of the scan lines used to compose the image. Sony Trinitron technology uses the aperture grille system.

Monitors featuring shadow mask technology often use an Invar shadow mask. Invar is a special metal that has an exceptionally low expansion rate. Monitors some-times experience displacement distortion when the shadow mask heats up, which affects color purity. An Invar shadow mask reduces this problem.

One of the most important monitor specifications is dot pitch. Dot pitch is the distance between the adjacent red/green/blue phosphor groups on the face of the CRT. The smaller the dot pitch, the sharper the image. Better monitors have a dot pitch of 0.28 mm and lower.

12.2 Troubleshooting the CRT

There are many different ways to check out a CRT. Some tests demand specialized equipment, such as a CRT tester, others can be done with a DMM or pattern generator. In this section, we explain how to perform these tests.

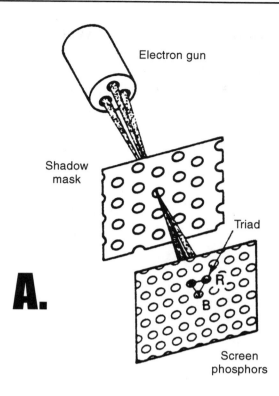

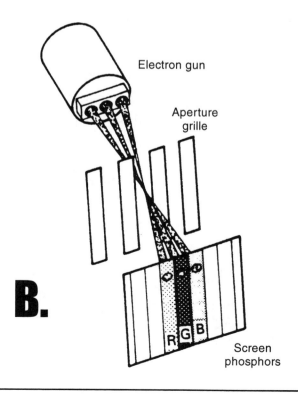

Figure 12.3. As electrons travel from the cathode to the phosphorescent face of the CRT, they pass through either a) a shadow mask or b) an aperture grille.

Using a CRT Tester

If you suspect a problem with a CRT and you have a CRT tester such as described in Chapter 2, you can check the condition of the CRT, each gun separately. If you find that there is a short between the grids and the filament, which is a common problem, then you can try to burn away that short with the tester. If you are successful, you can prolong the life of the CRT.

You may find that the three guns are not emitting electrons at the same level. In other words, one gun has a higher emission than another (the guns have to be within 10% of each other). You can try to *clean* one of the cathodes of the picture tube by applying a voltage to it. This voltage burns the oxide accumulation on the cathode so that it can again release a large quantity of electrons. Cleaning is a low-power process.

If cleaning doesn't help, you can try *rejuvenation*. Rejuvenation applies an even stronger voltage to the cathode. This may be successful, but may also make matters worse. If a picture tube is completely worn out, it is impossible to rejuvenate it. In this case, the only solution is to replace the CRT. One of the case studies shows how we used a CRT tester to clean the cathodes of a monitor's CRT.

Measuring CRT Voltages

Any time you suspect a problem with the CRT, you should measure its working voltages. This will help you decide if the CRT is at fault. The trouble may be caused by one or more voltages supplied to the CRT.

If the voltages are not correct, the image on the CRT display will look bad.

You must pay close attention to the level of the voltages on the CRT pins. You need to know the screen voltage on G2 and the focus voltage on G3. The focus voltage is very tricky to measure. You can't do it with a DMM, you need the proper tool—a high-voltage probe (see **Figure 12.4**). You also need to know the magnitude of the voltage that goes to the anode of the CRT. You need a high-voltage probe for this measurement, too. You can't measure this voltage with a DMM; it will explode in your hands.

The screen voltage is the most important. It can make the screen look very bright or very dark. It has to be around 400 volts. This voltage can be adjusted with the screen control located on the flyback. The screen voltage is the bottom control (see **Figure 12.5**). The top control is the focus voltage.

The anode charges the whole inside front portion of the picture tube, so that it accelerates the beam. The electrons released from the cathode need energy to travel the distance to the face of the CRT and strike the phosphor. The face of the CRT is at a positive voltage so it attracts the electrons.

Testing the Yoke

The yoke is actually a double coil consisting of horizontal and vertical deflection coils (see **Figure 12.6**). The horizontal coil has very low resistance, approximately 1 ohm. The vertical coil has a slightly higher resistance, approximately 14 to 24 ohms. This is the way to distinguish one coil from

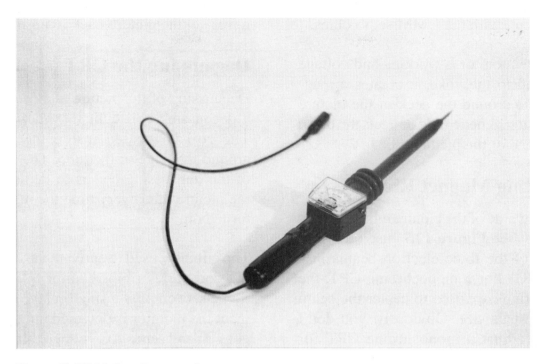

Figure 12.4. A high-voltage probe.

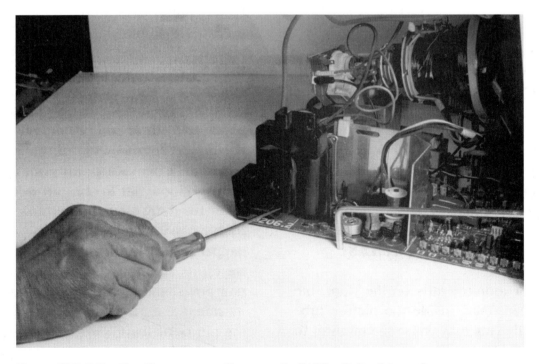

Figure 12.5. Adjusting the screen voltage control of the flyback transformer.

the other. Simply measure the resistance of each coil with the DMM set to ohms.

When the monitor is working and voltage is applied to the yoke, it creates a magnetic field around the neck of the picture tube. That magnetic field deflects the beam on the face of the picture tube.

Adjusting Magnet Rings

On the outside of the picture tube are magnet rings (see **Figure 12.7**) used for conversion of the three electron beams in a color CRT. For a monochrome CRT, the magnet rings are used to center the beam and adjust its size. Obviously, you don't have to adjust a monochrome CRT for color purity.

You need to be concerned about convergence if you change the picture tube or if you change the yoke. In other words, you'll have to deal with conversion if you disrupt the manufacturer's settings.

Adjusting the convergence in a CRT is a very tricky process. Additionally, the procedure varies from manufacturer to manufacturer. Basically, the procedure involves two steps: static convergence and dynamic convergence. If you want to do the adjustment correctly, you really should purchase the service manual for the monitor you are repairing. The service manual explains this process in detail (see **Figure 12.8**).

If a color monitor falls on the floor, the thin screen mask inside the picture tube may bend. This may cause the monitor to lose its purity or convergence. If this happens, the CRT is beyond repair. Everything

else may be working fine, but you can never get the picture back to normal.

Degaussing the CRT

Degaussing of the picture tube is done by a degaussing coil built into the monitor. The coil is located inside the cabinet around the edge of the tube. The purpose of the degaussing coil is to demagnetize the picture tube every time the monitor is turned on.

The circuitry used to activate the degaussing coil varies from monitor to monitor. Some sets employ a small relay. The moment the monitor is powered up, the relay goes on and sends AC voltage through the coil through a voltage dependent resistor (VDR). Other monitors use only the VDR. The surge of power goes through the VDR to the coil. The heavy surge increases the value of the VDR and stops the current flow. **Figure 12.9** shows the VDR in the Magnavox monitor.

In some other monitors, there is a switch either in the front or in the rear. On these monitors, demagnetizing can be done manually if there is a problem with color purity. Pressing the control sends voltage through the demagnetizing coil.

After finishing a repair, you may notice a problem with the color purity. As often happens during a repair, you turn the monitor on its side to work on the chassis. If you power the monitor with the CRT on its side, the Earth's magnetic field affects the purity of the CRT—it becomes magnetized. Then, you may notice one green spot and one blue spot on the display. You

Figure 12.6. The yoke is actually a double coil consisting of horizontal and vertical deflection coils.

Figure 12.7. Magnet rings are used for conversion of the three electron beams in a color CRT.

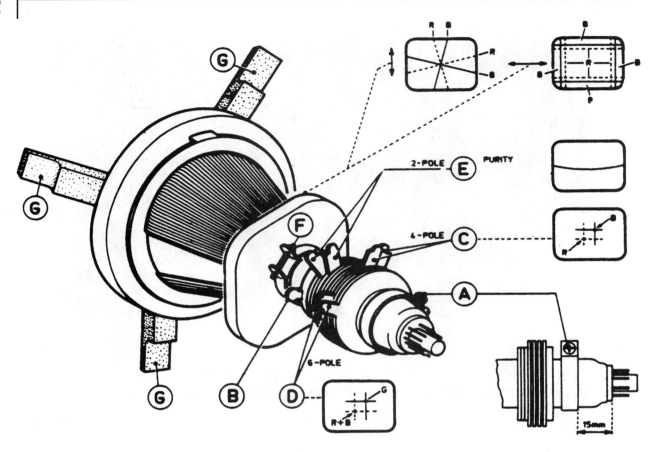

Figure 12.8. An example of the manufacturer's guidelines for adjusting static and dynamic convergence.

shouldn't be concerned with this distortion until you finish the repair.

Once you finish the repair, make sure the monitor's degaussing coil is connected to the printed circuit board. This is a small plug that connects to the printed circuit board near the power supply. If you have your own demagnetizing coil, you can use it to clear up the picture. Thereafter, the monitor's built-in coil will take care of the purity of the color.

Troubleshooting the CRT Socket

It's rare, but sometimes the focus lead of the CRT socket burns. When this happens,

the picture becomes very blurred. No matter how much you try to adjust the focus, you can't do it. The burn spot acts like a load for the control that adjusts the focus. If you suspect that the focus control is not working, it's a good idea to disconnect the focus lead from the CRT socket. Normally, there is a small cover with two latches that you can pry open with a small screwdriver. Once the latches are open, you can see if the spot is burned or not.

If the spot is not burned, then the problem is with the focus control. If it is burned, there are two things you can do. One is to scrape the burn spot and apply a little silicone (this helps most of the time). If the burn is too extensive, you have to replace

Figure 12.9. The VDR (voltage dependent resistor) in the Magnavox monitor.

the socket of the picture tube. This is not an expensive part and is not too difficult to replace.

If the lead that goes to the focus is in good condition—that is, there is no burn spot—then the flyback is defective and must be replaced. As mentioned earlier in the book, the focus control cannot be separated from the rest of the flyback transformer.

Other CRT Repair Techniques

If you have tried to clean or rejuvenate a CRT without success, you may want to try another approach. You can use a small transformer to increase the filament voltage from 6.3 volts to about 7 volts. This way, the weak cathode of the picture tube will be heated to a higher temperature and will release more electrons. Although this

technique might improve the picture, it is only a temporary fix.

Here is another technique you may want to try in a pinch. Most monitors use a filament voltage that is derived from the secondary of the flyback transformer. Sometimes, you may have a short between the filament and one of the cathodes, for example, the green cathode. If this happens, the green color will be out of control because the filament is changing the bias. The best thing to do in a case like this is to eliminate the bias caused by the shorted filament. To do this, you have to cut the CRT socket adapter from the copper side of the CRT board. Then, you have to attach a small isolation transformer in between the copper trace and the CRT socket. This isolation transformer is very similar to a booster transformer. The only difference is that the isolation transformer not only provides the voltage, but it separates the filament of the CRT from the secondary of the flyback transformer. There is no physical connection. This way, even though there is a short between the cathode and the filament, the bias doesn't change because the filament is no longer grounded.

Chapter 13

Troubleshooting Computer Monitor Controls

There are many ways to control the image you see on a computer monitor's screen. Some controls are accessible from outside the monitor, meant to be adjusted by the end-user. Others are internal controls, meant to be adjusted by a technician. If the controls are working, you can use them to keep the monitor in peak operating condition. If not, you have to know how to repair them, since a defective control can render the monitor useless.

We have already covered many of the computer monitor controls, especially in Chapters 9 and 10. In this chapter, we cover analog and digital controls in general, and then a few specific controls not covered earlier in the book.

13.1 Checking Analog Controls

Analog controls can be either external or internal controls. If external, an analog control may be a knob or wheel that turns a potentiometer. If internal, an analog control is usually a small potentiometer that can be adjusted with a small screwdriver (see **Figure 13.1**). All the controls of the Magnavox 6CM320974I are analog controls. These are clearly marked on the printed circuit board and also in the service manual.

Some controls work only in certain video modes. In the Magnavox, for example, the vertical amplifier operates in four different video modes (see **Figure 13.2**). There are four different potentiometers for the four different modes. In case there is any

Figure 13.1. An internal analog control is often a small potentiometer that can be adjusted with a small screwdriver.

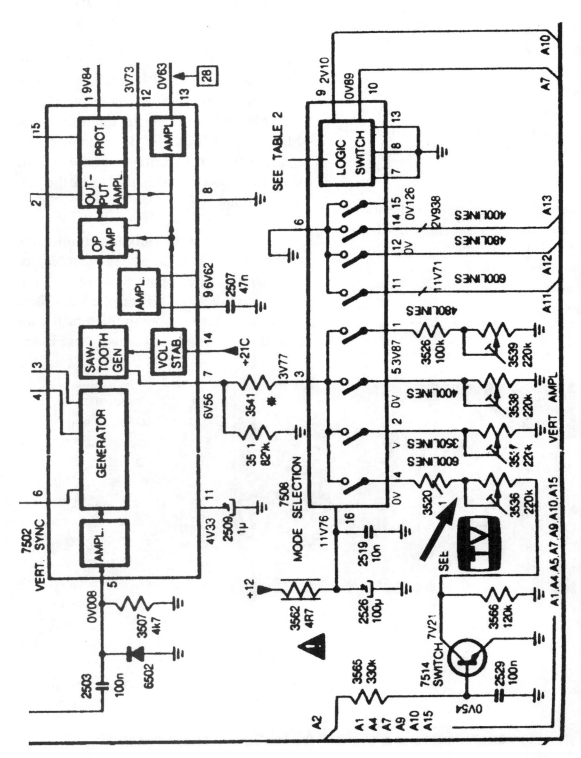

Figure 13.2. In the Magnavox monitor, the vertical amplifier operates in four different video modes. There are four different potentiometers for the four different modes.

trouble with one of the modes, the control can be very easily adjusted. But you need to be aware of the mode of operation. You should not adjust the controls that do not affect the current mode of operation.

A problem occurred with the horizontal width control of the Magnavox monitor. As you can see from the diagram in **Figure 13.3**, there is a separate amplifier for the horizontal width with separate controls, because the horizontal width varies according to the mode of operation. The horizontal width control is a 2-transistor circuit. Transistor 7512 is the output and transistor 7511 is the driver. These two transistors go to the horizontal yoke. Depending on the horizontal frequency at which the oscillator is running, transistor 7511 takes a signal from either transistor 7509 or 7513. To adjust the horizontal size, you turn either potentiometer 3554 (31.5 kHz) or 3546 (37.8 kHz).

If you turn a control and nothing happens, you can be sure that there is a problem somewhere in the circuit. The first component to check is the output transistor, since it is the most heavily stressed component of that circuit. In general, this is good troubleshooting practice: start from the end of the circuit. First, check the output transistor. If this is okay, check the driver transistor. If this is okay, check the switching transistor. Eventually, you will find a problem with a transistor, resistor or other component. Of course, the problem may lie with the control itself. Controls rarely break down completely, but sometimes they have problems. For example, they get dirty. You have to spray them with contact cleaner, and lubricate

them a little bit. Be gentle with small potentiometers. Don't force them, because they break easily.

13.2 Checking Digital Controls

Both the NEC Multisync 4D and Samtron SC-728SXL have digital controls. These are external controls available to the end-user. Both monitors also have analog controls, but we will concentrate on the digital controls here.

Monitors with digital controls employ pushbutton switches, which are typically located on the front panel (see **Figure 13.4**). These pushbuttons connect to a microprocessor, usually located on the main PC board or a separate control board. **Figure 13.5** shows the microprocessor in the NEC Multisync 4D. The output of the microprocessor is a digital signal that is converted to an analog voltage. This voltage increases or decreases according to the length of time the button is depressed (until maximum or minimum v1alues are reached). This voltage is then applied to a particular circuit to make the required adjustment. So, instead of turning a potentiometer control to change the voltage that goes to a certain circuit, pressing a pushbutton control (closing a switch) sends a digital signal to the microprocessor. The microprocessor then sends a signal to a digital-to-analog converter, which in turn produces an appropriate voltage that goes to the circuit that it controls. The same effect is accomplished in a different way.

If you have a problem with digital controls, there is a possibility that the microprocessor is bad, but it is more likely that one of the pushbutton switches is stuck or dirty.

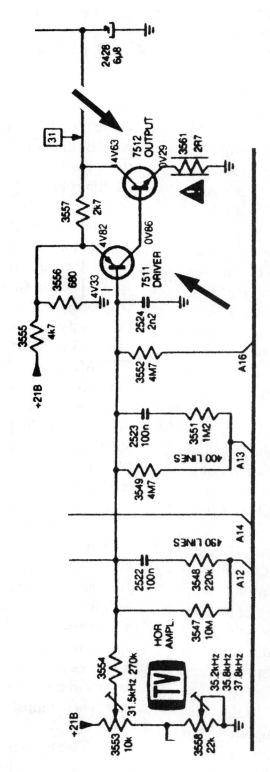

Figure 13.3. In the Magnavox monitor, the horizontal width control is a 2-transistor circuit.

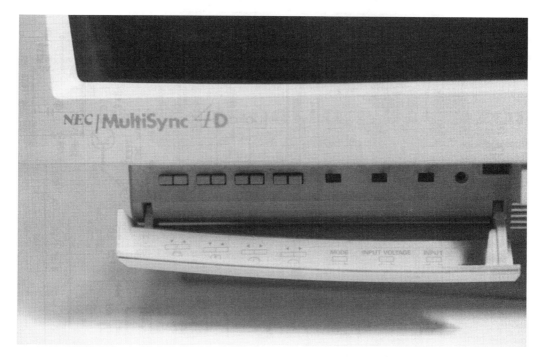

Figure 13.4. Monitors with digital controls employ pushbutton switches, which are typically located on the front panel.

Figure 13.5. The microprocessor in the NEC Multisync 4D resides on a daughterboard that connects to the main PC board of the monitor.

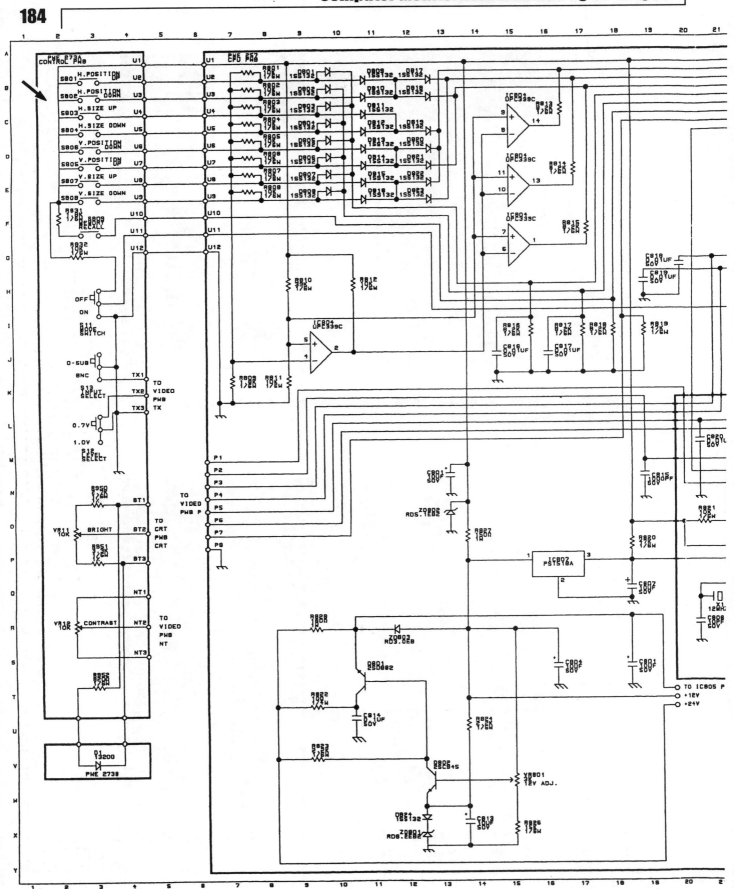

Figure 13.6. In the NEC Multisync 4D, when you press a control button, the signal goes through resistors and diodes to the input lines of the microprocessor, IC801.

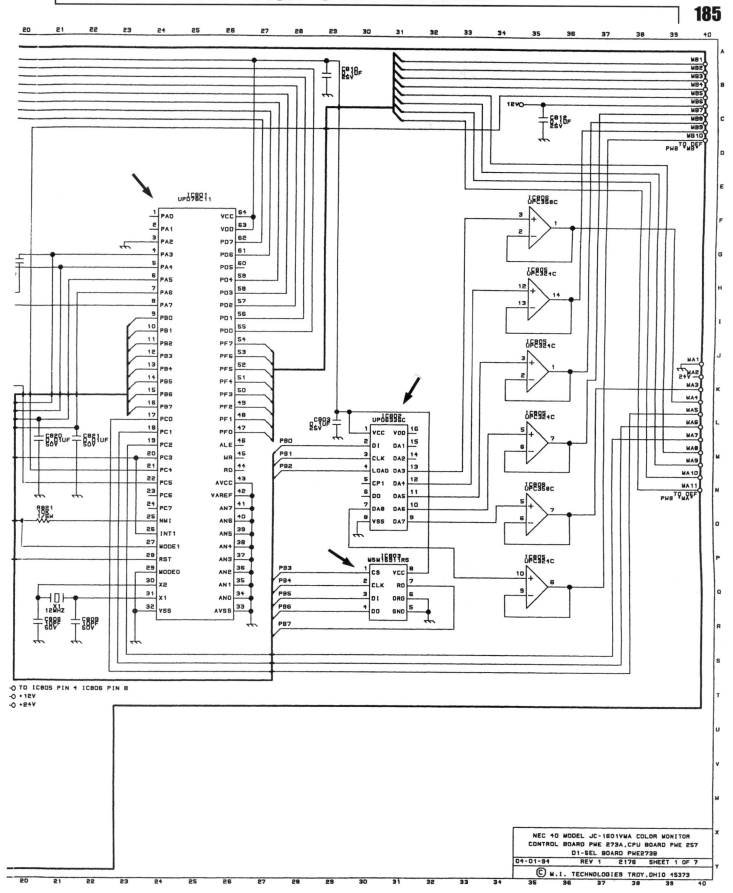

NEC 4D MODEL JC-1601VMA COLOR MONITOR
CONTROL BOARD PWE 273A, CPU BOARD PWE 257
D1-SEL BOARD PWE273B

| 04-01-94 | REV 1 | 2176 | SHEET 1 OF 7 |

© M.I. TECHNOLOGIES TROY, OHIO 45373

To make a quick check of a pushbutton switch, gently push it in. You should hear and feel the distinctive click of the switch. If you feel the click, the pushbutton is most likely in working condition.

The microprocessor accepts only one input at a time, so if one control is stuck in the on position, none of the other controls will work. This is because the microprocessor is working on the command that is pressed (stuck). Microprocessors used in computer monitors typically cannot handle both commands simultaneously.

If a pushbutton switch is dirty, it will not make contact. You have to take out the switch and measure it with a DMM set to measure ohms. This will tell you if the switch is making contact or not. If the switch measures infinite resistance when you push it in, it is not making contact. If dirt is the cause, you have to clean it with

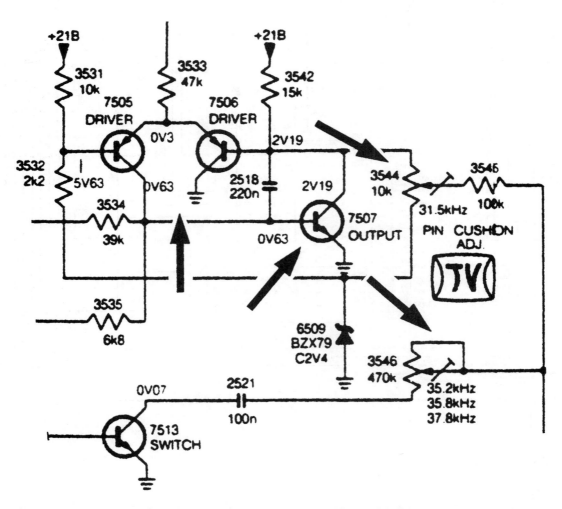

Figure 13.7. In the Magnavox monitor, the pincushion circuit employs a push-pull driver combination made up of transistors 7505 and 7506.

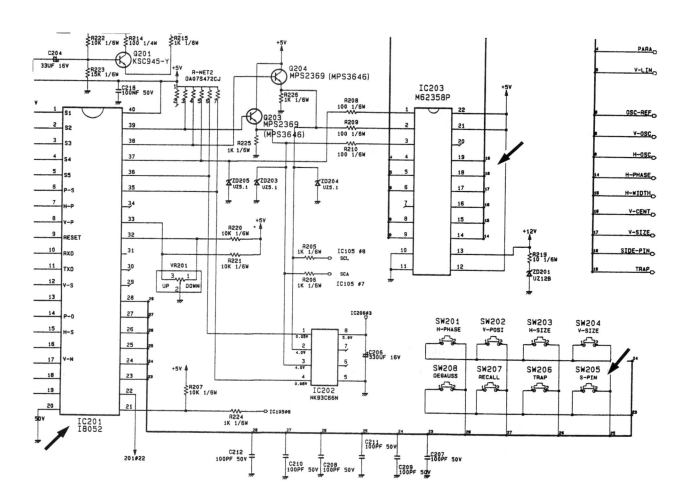

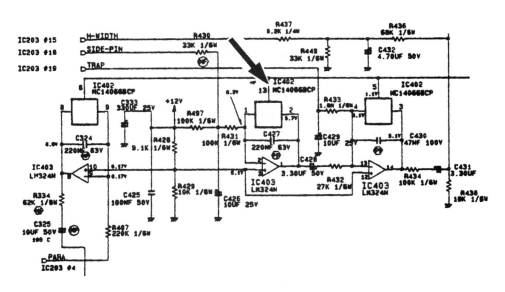

Figure 13.8. In the Samtron monitor, the pincushion control sends a voltage to the input of digital switch IC402 and op-amp IC403.

contact cleaner. If the switch is broken mechanically, then you have to replace it.

In the NEC Multisync 4D, when you press a button down, the signal goes through resistors and diodes to the input lines of the microprocessor, IC801 (see **Figure 13.6**). The signal comes out in digital form and goes to the digital-to-analog converter, IC802. This IC converts the digital signal to a voltage. The analog voltage is fed to an operational amplifier. From the op amp, the signal goes to the appropriate circuits in the monitor, for example, vertical or horizontal size. By raising or lowering the voltages, the picture shrinks or expands.

One other IC should be mentioned, IC803. This memory IC, an electrically erasable programmable read only memory (EEPROM), remembers the current settings so that you don't have to adjust the monitor every time you turn it on.

Although the external controls in the NEC make use of a microprocessor (digital controls for the user), many of the internal controls use potentiometers, which are on the main board, on the CRT board, and so forth. This is how the technician can fine tune the monitor.

13.3 Checking the Pincushion Control

The pincushion control takes care of any bowing that may occur at the right and left sides of the picture on the monitor's display. When this circuit is working, adjusting the potentiometer or pressing the digital control will bring the picture back to its proper rectangular shape. If you find that this control is not working, you have to check the transistors and related voltages and controls of the pincushion circuit.

In the Magnavox monitor, the pincushion circuit is a completely analog internal control (see **Figure 13.7**). This circuit employs a push-pull driver combination made up of transistors 7505 and 7506. The signal is fed to output transistor 7507. The pincushion adjustment potentiometer is either 3545 or 3546, depending on the video mode.

In the Samtron monitor, the pincushion control is an external pushbutton digital control on the front panel of the monitor. The circuit is shown in **Figure 13.8**. This control goes to the microprocessor, IC201, and then to the digital-to-analog converter, IC203, where it exits at pin 18. This voltage then serves as the input to digital switch IC402 and op amp IC403. To troubleshoot problems with this control, you need to check that the voltage varies at pin 18 of IC203 when the front panel switch is depressed. If this voltage is changing, the next points to check are the outputs of IC402 and IC403 to make sure they are working properly.

13.4 Checking the Brightness and Contrast Controls

The brightness control of a computer monitor changes the level of the voltage of the first grid of the CRT. This is done with a potentiometer. By turning the pot, you change the value of the voltage that goes to the first grid, normally between 20 and

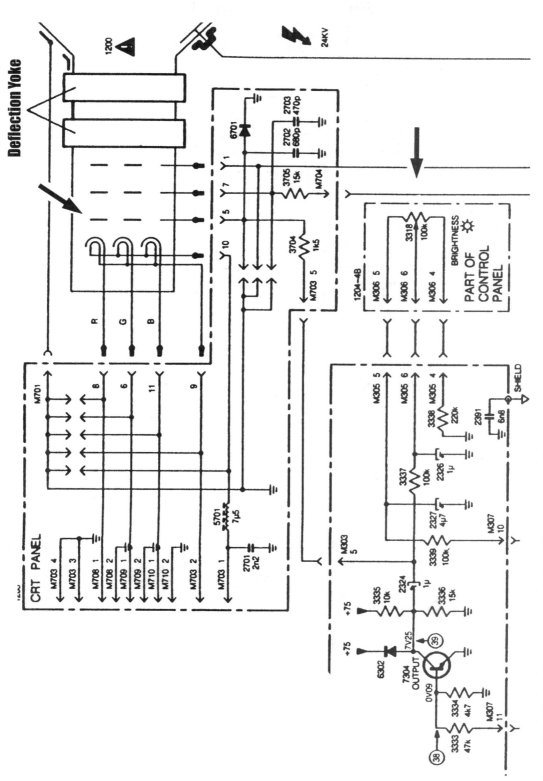

Figure 13.9. The brightness control of the Magnavox monitor.

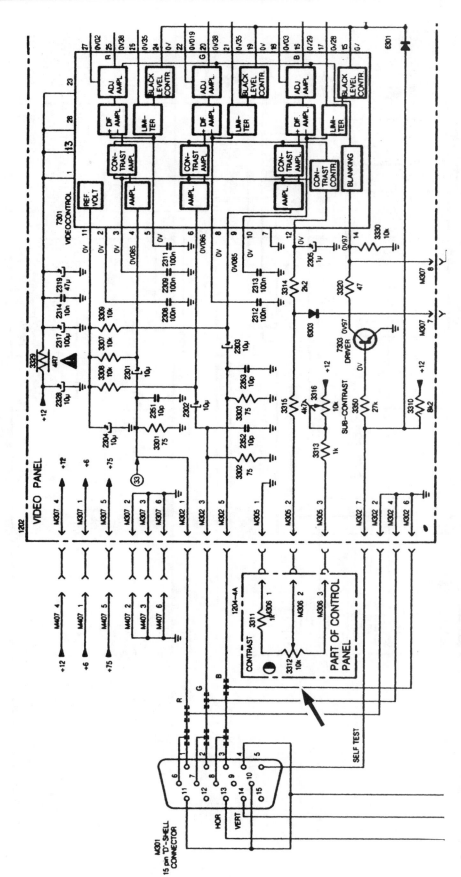

Figure 13.10. The contrast control of the Magnavox monitor.

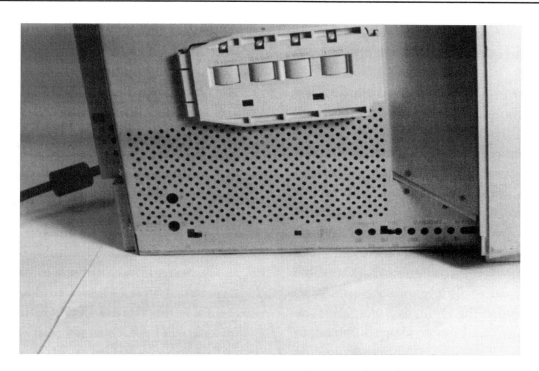

Figure 13.11. The brightness and contrast controls on the side of the Magnavox monitor.

50 volts. At 50 volts, the picture is darkest; at 20 volts, the picture is brightest.

The brightness control does not affect the level of the video signal that goes to the picture tube. In other words, brightness directly controls the picture tube's capacity to produce more light.

The contrast control actually changes the level of the video signal. If you keep the level of the contrast constant and increase the brightness, eventually the picture becomes washed out and very dim. There must be a balance between the contrast and the brightness to obtain the most acceptable picture. The brightness and contrast controls of the Magnavox are shown in **Figure 13.9** and **Figure 13.10**. These are

the analog controls on the side of the monitor (see **Figure 13.11**).

13.5 Checking the Focus Control

The display of a brand new computer monitor is very sharp. You can see all the details. Over the years, the CRT wears down and the picture loses its focus slowly but steadily. After years of service, the display can become blurred. This is most noticeable when text is on the screen. For example, lower case m's and n's and numbers like 3 and 4 may appear blurry.

Sometimes you can successfully adjust the focus, sometimes not. It depends on the condition of the CRT. Typically, the focus adjustment is an internal control, not available on the outside of the monitor.

Once you remove the cover, you can locate the focus adjustment on the body of the flyback transformer. As mentioned, this component contains two controls. The top control is for the focus, the bottom control is for the screen voltage.

Before adjusting the focus, you should put a test page on the screen, for example a page of number 4's or letter m's. Then, use a screwdriver to slowly turn the control to the left and to the right. By watching the screen go from blurry to sharp and back to blurry again, you will be able to gauge the maximum sharpness of the CRT. If the sharpness is acceptable, leave the control in that position. This is all you need to do to adjust the focus.

If you cannot get a decent sharpness, it means either the picture tube is worn out beyond adjustment or the flyback transformer focus control is burned out. If the latter is the case, you have no other choice but to change the flyback transformer.

One other problem can crop up. You may achieve an acceptable focus adjustment, but it will not remain in focus for very long—maybe a few days. This is also an indication that the flyback transformer needs to be replaced.

The focus actually is a voltage that goes from the flyback transformer through a resistor divider network. The level is about 5,000 volts. Through the focus control, you change the value of the voltage until you achieve the best possible sharpness.

13.6 Checking Color Alignment Controls

In order to produce color, a CRT has three electronic guns. In theory, the three guns are exactly the same, but in reality, there are slight differences. To compensate for these differences, the manufacturer always provides color controls. **Figure 13.12** shows the color controls that reside on the video board in the Magnavox monitor.

To make the adjustment, you need either a software program or a tool like the Checker-12 that provides a gray background pattern. Once the pattern is on the screen, you can make any adjustments necessary to bring the color on the monitor to absolute gray.

It is very difficult, if not impossible, to do a color alignment by displaying colors on the CRT. The alignment has to be done with the gray background, without any trace of color in the picture. The color controls are potentiometers located either on the video board or the CRT board in the computer monitor.

Figure 13.12. Color controls reside on the video board in the Magnavox monitor.

Chapter 14

Troubleshooting Microprocessor Circuits

In a computer monitor, the microprocessor has two important jobs. One is to monitor the frequencies of the horizontal and vertical sync pulses coming from video circuits in the computer and then generate the signals needed to adjust the display. This provides a monitor with its multiscanning capability. The other is to check the signals coming from the controls on the front panel and to adjust the display accordingly.

Not all monitors employ a microprocessor. For example, the Magnavox 6CM320974I does not have a microprocessor. However, both the NEC Multisync 4D and Samtron SC-728SXL use microprocessors.

The microprocessor performs other operations, too. For example, it controls the on-screen display, if the monitor has one, and can shut down certain parts of the power supply. **Figure 14.1** shows a block diagram of the microprocessor and its support circuits in the Samtron monitor.

The D/A converter and the EEPROM chip comprise the circuits that work with the microprocessor. The microprocessor accepts inputs from the video circuits in the computer and from the digital controls and sends signals to the D/A converter. The D/A converter changes the digital signals to analog voltages. The EEPROM stores the current settings of the monitor. Any time a change is made in the monitor settings, the microprocessor updates the settings in the EEPROM.

14.1 Checking the Microprocessor

Don't expect to have many problems with the microprocessor, because this is a low-power circuit. If you do suspect a problem, it's fairly easy to check out the microprocessor. First of all, you have to check the clock signal of the microprocessor. The frequency of the clock is usually determined by an external crystal. This frequency is marked on the crystal. In this case, the crystal, X201, has a frequency of 12 MHz (see **Figure 14.2**). If you have a

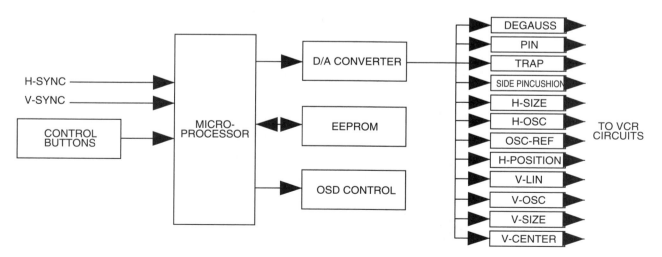

Figure 14.1. A block diagram of the microprocessor and its support circuits in the Samtron monitor.

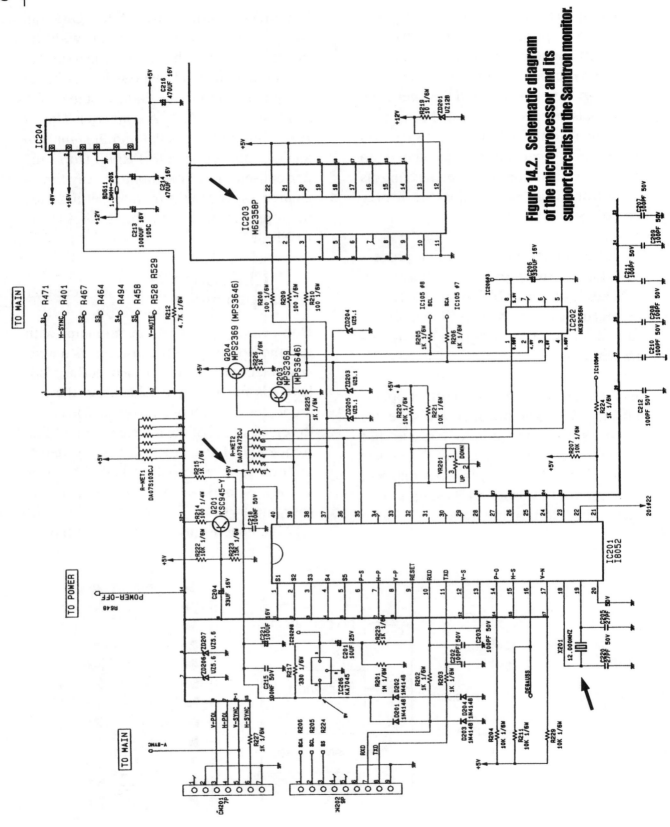

Figure 14.2. Schematic diagram of the microprocessor and its support circuits in the Samtron monitor.

frequency counter, you can measure the frequency. If the clock is working at 12 MHz, that's a good indication. It doesn't mean that the microprocessor is working, but at least it is receiving the correct clock signal.

The next test is to check if the microprocessor is getting power. Most computer monitor microprocessors operate with a 5 volt power supply. In the Samtron, microprocessor IC201 receives 5 volts at pin 40. The ground pin is pin 20. If the voltage at pin 40 measures approximately 5 volts, this is another good sign. The microprocessor is receiving power.

The next test is to check if the incoming signals are present. For example, when you press one of the pushbuttons on the front panel, is there any change in the status,

high or low, at the appropriate pin of the microprocessor. You can check this with a logic probe or a DMM. The final test is to check if there are any outputs coming from the microprocessor. If the outputs are working, the microprocessor is good.

14.2 Checking the Digital-to-Analog Converter

If the monitor is still experiencing a problem, for example, with one of the controls , the next component to check is the digital-to-analog converter. This IC changes the voltage, depending on how long you press the front panel button. If the voltages are not changing, then the converter is at fault (IC203 in the Samtron). Beyond this point, the trouble is with the analog circuitry rather than the microprocessor and its support circuits.

Chapter 15

Troubleshooting Power Supply Circuits

The power supply of a computer monitor is the source of many electrical problems. Why is this so? The power supply is subject to many of the conditions that make electronic components unreliable. Electrical surges and heat are two prime examples. The power supply usually takes the brunt of any electrical surge in the AC line. It takes the first punch, in a sense. Heat buildup in the power supply often dries out capacitors, causing them to fail. If you turn on the power of a computer monitor and see no response (the display does not come on), check whether the monitor is plugged in. If it is, you need to check if there is a problem with the power supply.

In this chapter, we cover the two most common types of power supplies: linear and switch mode. We'll cover the switch mode supply in greater detail, since this type of supply is more prevalent in today's computer monitors.

15.1 Linear Power Supplies

Linear power supplies are an older type of supply, but are still used in some computer monitors. Linear power supplies are not very efficient and weigh a lot, but they are easy to build and reliable.

The linear supply employs a standard step-down transformer. The transformer serves two functions. It lowers the voltage, and it provides isolation between the primary side, which is connected to the AC line, and the secondary side. If more than one voltage is needed by the equipment, the secondary of the transformer will have several secondary windings that produce different voltages. This is the case with all computer monitors.

On the secondary winding side of the transformer can be bridge, full-wave and half-wave rectifiers. The bridge rectifier is the most efficient, allowing a smaller filter capacitor to be used. Most computer monitors with linear supplies use all three kinds of rectifiers.

A bridge rectifier is constructed with four diodes. These diodes may be discrete, or housed in a single package that looks like an integrated circuit. A full-wave rectifier is constructed with two diodes. A half-wave rectifier employs just one diode. All three types rectify the AC and produce a DC voltage. This DC voltage is filtered by a capacitor and then fed to a regulator, which regulates the outgoing voltage.

The supply may have one or more voltage regulators, depending a the number of voltages required for operation of the equipment. Connected to the output of each regulator is a capacitor typically rated at between 10 and 50 microfarads. The reason for this capacitor is that the voltage needs to be filtered. The capacitor filters out any ripple in the voltage.

The filtered voltages from the regulators are then applied to the various circuits in the computer monitor.

When repairing a monitor, if you notice that the fuse is blown on the primary side of the power supply, it means that the transformer is taking excessive current. It is not wise to just replace the fuse and power up the monitor again. It's a good idea to check the full-wave rectifier, diodes and zener diodes on the secondary side of the transformer. If one of these components shorts out, excessive current flows to ground and blows the fuse.

Problems in a linear power supply are fairly easy to spot. With a DMM set to the ohmmeter range, you can measure each component to find out if there are any shorts. The repair work is straightforward. It is not something that requires special tools or test equipment. All you have to do is desolder the shorted component and replace it with a new one.

15.2 Switch Mode Power Supplies

Switch mode power supplies do the same kind of job as linear supplies, but in a different, more efficient, way. In a linear supply, first there is a transformer, then a rectifier, then a regulator. In a switch mode supply, first there is a rectifier, then a transformer. Regulation in a switch mode supply is accomplished by feeding back part of the output to the input. The transformers used in switch mode supplies are called flyback transformers or switch mode transformers. They are much lighter than the transformers used in linear supplies. **Figure 15.1** shows the schematic diagram of the switch mode power supply in the NEC Multisync 4D. **Figure 15.2** shows how the supply is positioned in the monitor.

In a switch mode power supply, 120 volts AC from the electrical line passes through an rf filter and is fed to a bridge rectifier (D611 in the schematic). This converts the voltage to approximately 150 volts DC. This high voltage is converted back to AC by a switching transistor, in this case,

Q601. A switching transistor turns on and off, on and off, thus producing the AC voltage. This voltage is fed to the flyback or switch mode transformer (T601). The secondary of this transformer produces several different voltages, which are rectified by three half-wave rectifiers (D12, D13, D14) and made available to the various circuits of the monitor.

In a switch mode power supply, regulation is accomplished by controlling the ratio of the on-time to off-time of the switching transistor. This is done through feedback circuitry. In the NEC monitor, deviations in the secondary voltages are detected by transistor Q602 through reference zener diodes ZD602, ZD603 and ZD604. The output of Q602 controls the current though the photodiodes of optoisolators PC601 and PC602. This current changes the voltages at the emitters of the phototransistors of the optoisolators. Note in the schematic diagram of **Figure 15.1**, the optoisolator is shown in separate parts. Actually, these are two parts of the same component.

The difficulty in servicing switch mode power supplies stems from the fact that they are so-called *closed loop* circuits, because they use a feedback voltage.

The feedback voltages are fed to the gate of the switching transistor (Q601) through IC601. This IC controls the regulation of the on and off cycle (pulse width) of the switching transistor. This technique is called pulse width modulation (PWM). Controlling the pulse width determines how long the transistor will stay on and how long it stays off. This method adjusts the voltage in the secondary to be at a con-

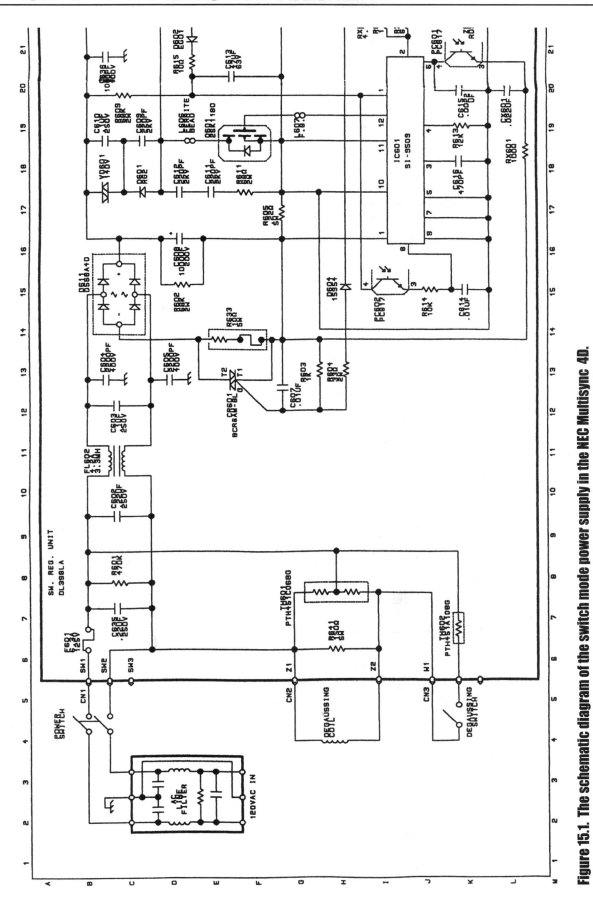

Figure 15.1. The schematic diagram of the switch mode power supply in the NEC Multisync 4D.

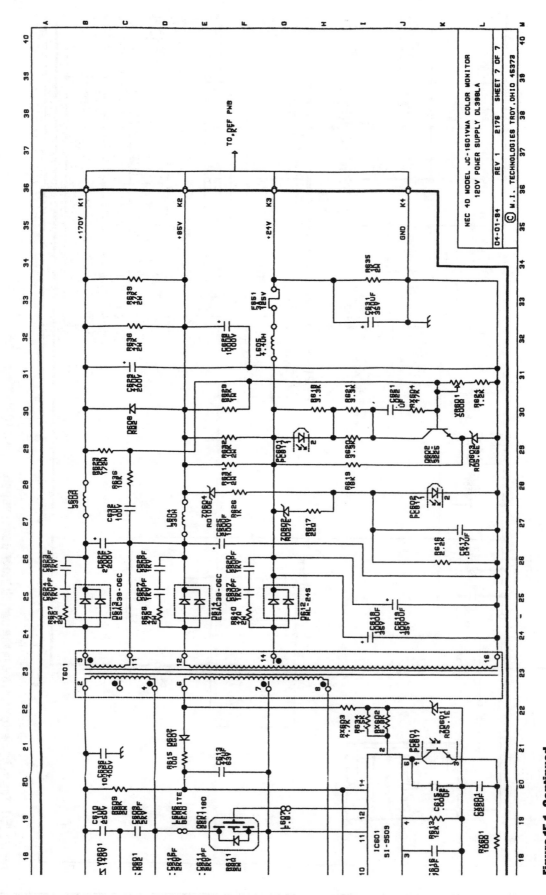

Figure 15.1. Continued.

Figure 15.2. The power supply in the NEC monitor resides on a separate PC board attached to the metal shield on the left side of the monitor.

stant level, which is preset by the reference voltage.

An optoisolator is used in the power supply because the primary of the power supply has a hot ground, which is connected to the electrical ground. The secondary has a separate ground. There is no way to communicate between the two grounds. The only way is with an optoisolator, which has a very high isolation voltage, about 5,000 volts. The feedback works through the optoisolator to adjust the outgoing voltage.

Why do you need feedback? When the switching transistor is on, energy is stored in the transformer. When the transistor is off, the energy from the transformer is released. This is the way the switch mode power supply works. When the load connected to the secondary increases, the switching control transistor extends the on time of the pulse so that the transistor stays

on longer. When the current drops down again, the on-time of the pulse is decreased, so the transistor stays off longer.

A typical problem in a computer monitor is a blown fuse. Replacing the fuse rarely solves the problem. Obviously, something has caused the fuse to blow.

The first component to check is the bridge rectifier. If this is okay, then check the switching transistor. The switching transistor can be damaged by lightning, by spikes in the electrical line, or by overloading. If the switching transistor is good, then you may either put in a new fuse or connect a 100 watt light bulb between the leads of the fuse holder (in place of the fuse) to see if the supply is going to work.

A switch mode power supply is a self-contained unit in many monitors. You may take the supply out of the monitor and service it separately on the bench. You don't need the rest of monitor, because all the voltages produced by the power supply are fairly independent from the load. If you use the light bulb and there is a problem in the feedback loop, the light bulb will light up. In a working power supply, the light bulb will be very dim; you will hardly see any light.

If there is no voltage in the secondary, then it is a little more difficult to service the supply, since all the voltages are interrelated. You have to start checking component by component; there is no other way. Check the switching transistor, check the IC, check the reference zeners, all the rectifiers in the secondary, and so on. There must be a reason that the power supply won't turn on.

Sometimes, there is a short in the secondary so the switching transistor never turns on. Sometimes, a rectifier in the secondary will short out, burn up a resistor, and destroy the switching transistor. Sometimes, but rarely, the optoisolator or one of the error detector transistors goes bad.

Capacitors sometimes dry up and don't rectify the secondary voltage, so there is no feedback coming to the optoisolator. These capacitors in the secondary are most likely to fail. The capacitors are warmed by the heat from the transformer and the heatsink of the switching transistor when the monitor is operating. After years of operation, they may dry out. When they dry out, the voltage drops down and the reference voltage gets lost. Keep in mind, too, the whole power supply is often housed in a metal chassis, which tends to exacerbate the heat problem.

Switch mode supplies are not as simple to troubleshoot as linear supplies. For example, if capacitor C628 in the NEC power supply were to dry up, the 85 volts would be missing. Then, the power supply would not turn on, because the photodiode in the optoisolator would not be getting enough current, and the phototransistor would not change its value. Most of the time, by checking the components, you can locate the one that has failed.

Electronics parts suppliers sell kits for servicing switch mode power supplies. The kit includes all the components that go bad: capacitors, diodes, transistors. You can replace almost the whole supply with these new parts. This way you don't overlook anything. When replacing parts, you must pay close attention to the polarity of the capacitors and diodes. You have to install them properly.

Very rarely do you have to change the switch mode transformer. If you want to check this transformer, you will need special equipment, such as a Sencore computer monitor analyzer. Sencore has a patented ringing test, which tells you immediately if the transformer is good.

15.3 Power Management Circuits

Many monitors built in the past five to ten years include power management circuitry. Power management reduces operating costs, lowers consumption of natural resources, and extends the life of the monitor. Reducing power consumption during periods of inactivity is the goal of the EPA Energy Star program. Thus, you will notice that many monitors are Energy Star compliant.

EPA guidelines specify that a monitor consume less than 30 watts in the standby/suspend mode, and less than 15 watts in the off mode. VESA has issued uniform guidelines of display power management signaling (DPMS), to insure the monitor can respond to signals issued by the computer.

In a DPMS compliant monitor, removal of either vertical or horizontal sync signals from the video adapter causes the monitor to enter a standby/suspend mode. This shuts off the deflection and high voltage in the monitor, but the CRT filament remains lit. When system activity resumes, the display returns almost instantaneously.

Removal of both vertical and horizontal sync signals causes the monitor to enter a power-off mode, where the CRT heater is off, but the DPMS sense circuitry is active. This is the maximum power saving mode. If the user attempts to resume activity, several seconds will elapse before the display attains full brightness.

The time intervals of system input inactivity (no keystrokes or mouse movements) are set via software (as part of the video adapter's drivers in Microsoft Windows), a separate Terminate and Stay Resident program (TSR), or the PC BIOS. When a time interval exceeds the pre-determined setting, the computer system signals the video adapter, which, in turn, signals the monitor.

DPMS compliant monitors not only save energy when idle, but are less prone to surges because their power supplies are operational, even in the power-off mode. The supply needs to be ready to restore the display immediately from this low-power mode.

In the Samtron SC-728SXL, DPMS operation is handled by microprocessor IC201, voltage regulator IC204 and IC605, and transformer T603. The POWER-OFF signal is at pin 14 and the POWER-SUSPEND signal is at pin 6 of the microprocessor. The schematic diagram of the DPMS circuitry is shown in **Figure 15.3**. This circuitry in found in the power supply section, which is on the main printed circuit board in this monitor.

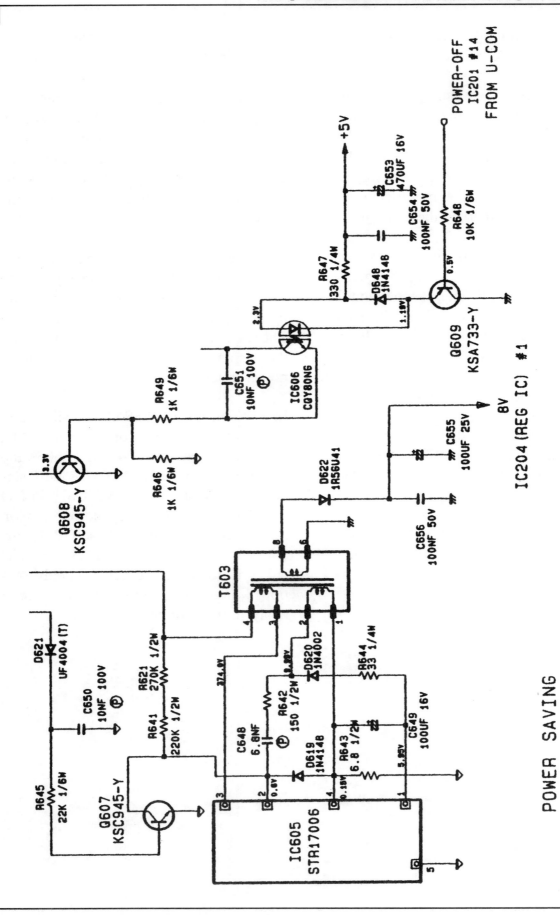

POWER SAVING

Figure 15.3. The schematic diagram of the DPMS circuitry in found in the Samtron monitor. This circuitry in found in the power supply section.

Chapter 16
Miscellaneous

16.1 Audio Circuits

As mentioned in Chapter 3, audio circuits in a personal computer system are found in the system unit rather than in the monitor. However, monitors that accept composite video also have inputs for audio. These are the monitors used years ago for Apple II+ and similar computers.

These monitors have simple audio circuits, which amplify a low-level signal of about 0.5 volts. After amplification, the signal is sent to the audio output circuit, which in most cases is a low-power integrated circuit. This IC delivers about 1.5 watts of power to a small speaker in the monitor's cabinet.

16.2 Locating Spare Parts

Computer monitor parts are general electronic parts. As such you can order these parts from most any good parts supplier. You should scour the area where you live for a good parts supplier. It's much better to be able to purchase parts in the vicinity of your shop, than to have to order from companies in another city or state. We use a parts supplier, East Coast Transistor, which is a national distributor, but happens to be located only five minutes from our repair shop.

But, we also use parts suppliers throughout the country. We have found that no single distributor can stock every part you might need for a repair. Some of our favorites are MAT Electronics, Parts Express, Dalbani, RNJ Electronics, Suburban Electronics Wholesalers, Electro Dynamics, Inc. (EDI), Digi-Key and Fox International. (Company listings can be found in

Appendix G at the back of the book.) All of these companies carry parts needed to service computer monitors, such as flyback transformers. It's wise to have five to ten catalogs on hand so that you can locate any spare part you might need.

You need to be careful when ordering parts. Make sure to ask if a part is in stock, and how fast the company can send the part to you. Try to become familiar with each company's policies for payment, returns, warranties and so forth. These policies are usually spelled out in the catalog. Finally, don't forget to check the price of the part. A price change may have occurred since the catalog was printed.

Certain parts, such as the flyback transformer, are specific to the particular monitor, and must be purchased from a supplier who sells the exact replacement part. Suburban Electronics Wholesalers, for example, stocks a good supply of flybacks. Some computer monitor parts, such as the signal cable, are very difficult to find. Dalbani is one company that carries this part.

Manufacturers also sell parts. If you want an exact replacement for an IC, a flyback or any other part, don't hesitate to contact the manufacturer. You may find, however, that parts are more expensive and are not shipped out as quickly as from independent parts suppliers.

We use the term *junkbox* whenever we refer to spare parts we have on hand. In our shop, we have plenty of old circuit boards which we have acquired over the years. Sometimes, when we need a resistor or capacitor, we desolder the part from one of these boards. If you take a resistor from an old board, make sure to check the resistance value with your DMM. You have to be careful with electrolytic capacitors. These capacitors have a tendency to dry out over the years. You need to be very selective with any capacitors you plan to use in a switch mode power supply. These capacitors are typically high temperature capacitors. A capacitor normally has a temperature rating of 85°C or 105°C. It's a good idea to install only capacitors with the higher temperature rating in a switch mode supply.

Some parts suppliers have their own Web sites, which makes it easy to search for parts. To access a Web site you need a personal computer with a modem and browser software plus an account with an Internet Service Provider (ISP) or an online service like America Online. For best results, we recommend a Pentium-class computer running under Microsoft Windows95. The modem should be 33.6K bps or faster. **Figure 16.1** shows the database search function of the Digi-Key Web site (www.digikey.com).

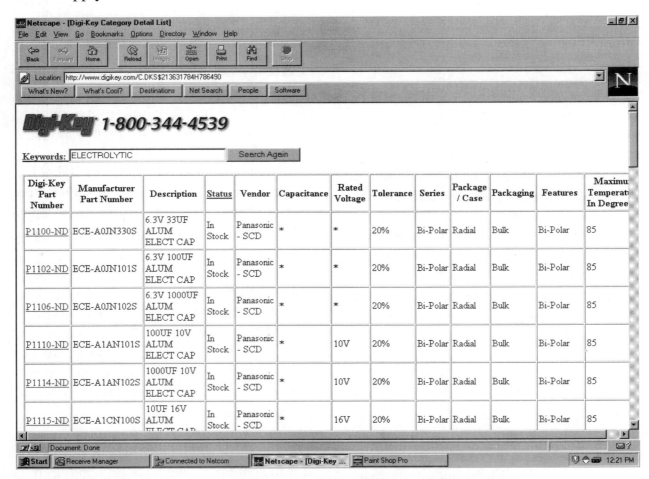

Figure 16.1. The database search function of the Digi-Key Web site (www.digikey.com).

16.3 Service Manuals

Service manuals can be an excellent source of information when repairing a monitor. A good service manual contains schematic diagrams of the monitor, parts layout diagrams, parts lists, alignment procedures, relevant waveforms for different points in the circuit, wiring diagrams, exploded views to aid in disassembly, monitor specifications, and general information.

It can become expensive, though, if you purchase a service manual for every monitor you repair. Service manuals run from around $20 to over $100, with the average about $35. Shipping charges also add to the cost. Standard shipping is not expensive, but takes a long time. Waiting for a service manual could add an additional week to the time needed to perform the repair.

Obviously, we ordered the service manuals for the three model monitors we described throughout the book. We ordered the service manual for the Magnavox 6CM320974I from the manufacturer, Philips Consumer Electronics Company. We tried to order the service manual for the NEC Multisync 4D from the manufacturer, but they did not have it in stock. So, we called International Components Marketing (ICM). They did not have the service manual, but did have the schematic diagram for this monitor. We also ordered the Samtron SC-728SXL service manual from ICM. We did this as a matter of convenience.

Both the Magnavox and Samtron service manuals are excellent. The Magnavox schematics include small icons to indicate

the different controls in the circuit. This is a great help when troubleshooting the monitor. The schematics, though, use a European way of denoting resistance and voltage values. A resistance of 2.2 kilohms, for example, is shown as 2k2, while a resistance of 2.2 ohms is shown as 2R2. For voltages, the schematic inserts a V in place of a decimal point. For example, 5V3 indicates 5.3 volts. A Samtron service manual has detailed schematics with references to large (1.25" x 1.75") scope printouts to help in understanding how waveforms are changing in the circuit. An example is shown in **Figure 16.2**. The Samtron manual also included several pages of troubleshooting flowcharts. An example is shown in **Figure 16.3**.

Both service manuals included exploded diagrams to indicate how the monitor should be disassembled. An example from the Samtron manual is shown in **Figure 16.4**.

The schematic diagram for the NEC Multisync 4D was just as expensive as the entire Samtron service manual ($45). And this schematic was not nearly as high quality as the schematics in the two service manuals. For example, some ICs were left out (presumably due to lack of space), and some circuit labels did not match from page to page. Nevertheless, this diagram was a great aid in completing the repair of this monitor. Remember, even if a schematic has mistakes or omissions, you can often determine the correct status of the circuit just by looking at the actual PC board.

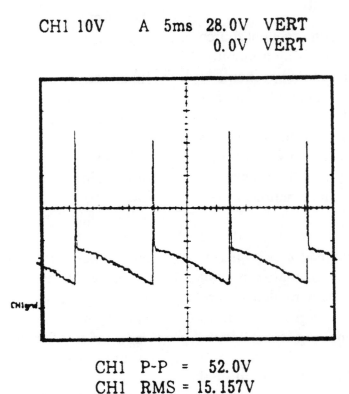

CH1 10V   A 5ms 28.0V   VERT
                   0.0V   VERT

CH1 P-P = 52.0V
CH1 RMS = 15.157V

Figure 16.2. An example of a scope printout from the Samtron service manual.

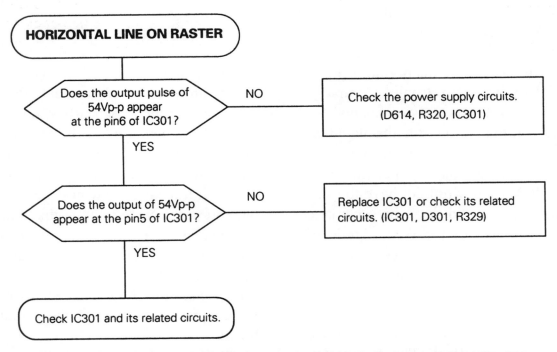

Figure 16.3. An example of a troubleshooting flowchart from the Samtron service manual.

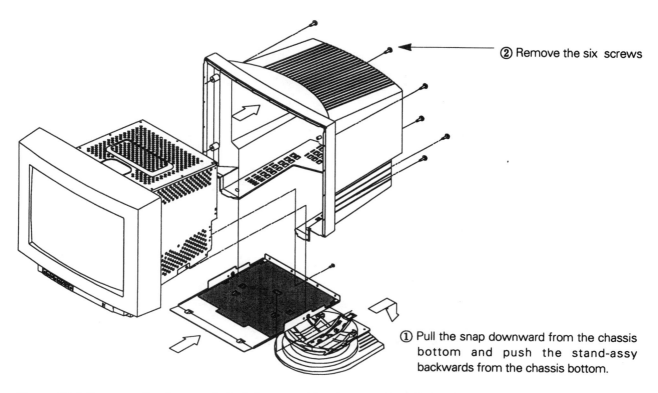

② Remove the six screws

① Pull the snap downward from the chassis bottom and push the stand-assy backwards from the chassis bottom.

Figure 16.4. An example of an exploded disassembly diagram from the Samtron manual.

If you don't want to purchase a service manual, you can examine it for free at any library that carries these reference materials. It is easier, however, to find service manuals for TVs and VCRs than for computer monitors.

Howard W. Sams & Co. is also a source for computer monitor schematics, though it has a limited listing.

Case Study 1:
Tatung Model CM-1498X

Our first case study concerns a Tatung Model CM-1498X SVGA monitor. This monitor had an obvious problem: it was completely dead. This symptom suggests a defective or blown component somewhere in the monitor's power supply, but this is not always the case.

We removed the rear cover from the monitor and looked for the power supply. This monitor employs a switch mode power supply in a shielded enclosure. We removed the enclosure and checked the fuse. The fuse looked good, but we checked for continuity with our DMM to make sure. The DMM confirmed that the fuse was good. This indicated that the problem was located outside the power supply. When there is a short outside the power supply—on the main printed circuit board, for example—the fuse does not blow, but the supply shuts down and does not deliver any power to the monitor.

If you suspect a short in the main circuitry, the first place to check is always the horizontal output transistor. This transistor works under a heavy load all the time. To check the transistor, you don't need to remove it from the circuit. All you need is clear access to the three leads of the transistor on the foil side of the PC board. In this monitor, when you turn the monitor on its side, you have excellent access to the foil side of the board.

How do you find the output transistor? Normally this transistor is in a TO-3PJ style case (see **Figure A.1**). This case is flat black with a metal tab. There is a hole in the tab for a screw. This transistor is always screwed to a heat sink, so it is rela-

tively easy to spot. Also, it is always located near the flyback transformer.

Here is how to measure for a shorted transistor. With the DMM set to the diode setting, measure between the collector, which is the middle pin, and the base or emitter pins. Never measure in-circuit between the base and emitter. The emitter is always connected to the secondary of the horizontal drive transformer, which has very low resistance. Measuring between the base and emitter in-circuit will always show a short.

We measured between the collector and base and found that the transistor, a 2SC3883, was shorted. We desoldered the transistor, unscrewed it from the heat sink, and pulled it out of the PC board with needle-nose pliers. We replaced this shorted transistor with a new one.

Even though we had replaced the shorted transistor, it was not time to turn on the power. A shorted transistor often causes damage to other components. We checked the main board for other shorts. This takes some time, but it is time well spent. The best approach is to measure the large com-

**Figure A.1.
Horizontal output
transistors are often
housed in a TO-3PJ style case.**

ponents, which are prone to failure because of the loads they carry. The components most likely to fail, besides the horizontal output transistor, are the vertical output transistor or IC, and voltage regulators. All of these components are easy to spot. They run hot and, therefore, are attached to heat sinks.

During our component checks, we found a shorted transistor, which had been working as a regulator, a 2SD1138 (ECG375). This transistor was difficult to get to, under the yoke of the picture tube. We removed it by desoldering not only the transistor pins but the heat sink pins, too. It would have been very difficult, if not impossible, to remove the screw that attaches the transistor to the heat sink. Instead, we removed the two pieces as a unit. In other words, we removed the transistor and heat sink at the same time. Once we had it out, we unscrewed the transistor from the heat sink and replaced it.

Reinstalling this transistor/heatsink combination was not easy. Five holes had to be aligned. The pins on the new transistor were, obviously, clean and free of solder. But the heat sink still had solder on its pins. The easiest way to remove this solder is to melt it and then, while holding the heatsink with pliers, hit the heatsink against the workbench. The solder will fly off the heatsink. This is what we did. Then we cleaned up the heatsink pins with a metal file. With all the pins free of solder, we were able to mount the transistor/heatsink combination into the PC board and solder all the pins into place.

At this point, we were satisfied that there were no more shorts. We now powered up the monitor to see if it would work. The monitor came on and the picture looked very good. We kept the monitor on and checked the condition of the output transistor. If there are any problems, this transistor will get very hot very fast. You should not touch the transistor while the set is on, because there is high voltage at this transistor. You can, however, touch the side of the heat sink—with dry fingers—to test the temperature. For increased safety, turn the set off first. In this case, the transistor was warm to the touch, as expected, but not excessively hot.

Before returning the set to normal operation, we adjusted the focus. This is done by turning the focus control located on the flyback transformer (the top control). To do this adjustment correctly, you have to put a test pattern up on the display. We use our test software for this purpose. After performing this adjustment, we reassembled the monitor. This completed the repair. **Figures A.2** through **A.9** show how the repair was done.

Step-by-Step Procedure...

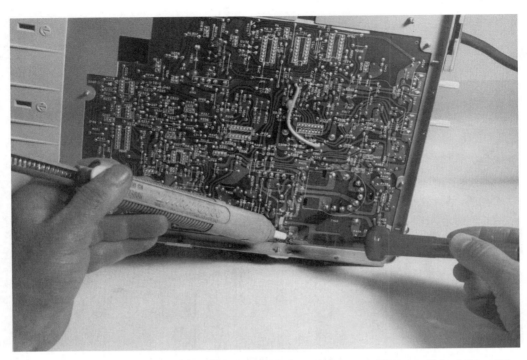

Figure A.2. After making a preliminary check of the horizontal output transistor with our DMM and finding a short, we desoldered the transistor from the main PC board.

Figure A.3. The horizontal output transistor is attached to a heatsink with a screw and nut. We used a nut driver to remove the nut and then removed the screw by hand.

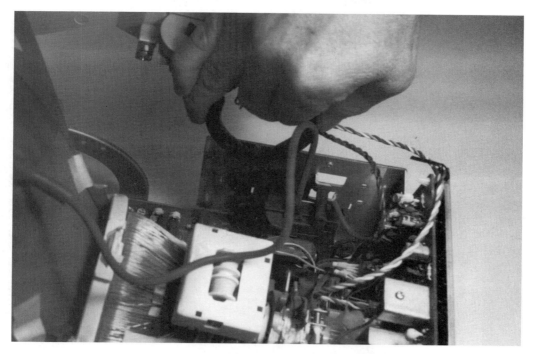

Figure A.4. Using needle-nose pliers to pull the horizontal output transistor out of the PC board.

Figure A.5. Re-checking the transistor with a DMM to confirm the short.

Figure A.6. After soldering the new horizontal output transistor back into place, we checked to make sure the transistor was good.

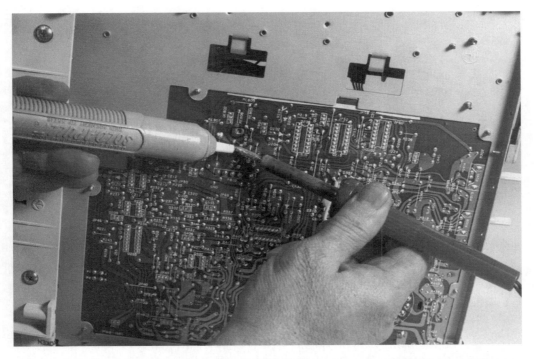

Figure A.7. Before placing the monitor back into operation we checked a few other components for shorts and found a shorted regulator. We desoldered the regulator along with the heat sink it was attached to and removed the two as one piece.

Figure A.8. Before re-assembling the monitor, we sharpened up the focus by adjusting the focus control on the flyback. This control is accessible through the large keyhole-shaped cutout in the metal plate at the lower left.

Figure A.9. The Tatung monitor back in operation.

Appendix B

Case Study 2:
Magnavox Model 6CM3209741

Our second case study concerns a Magnavox Model 6CM320974I SVGA monitor. This monitor was overscanning from side to side. In other words, the horizontal width control was not operating. This problem made the monitor unusable since the left and right sides of the display could not be viewed.

We began the repair by removing the rear cover of the monitor. We discovered that this monitor is heavily shielded to comply with emission standards. The shield completely covers all the monitor's electronics, making it impossible to make any measurements or repairs. We were forced to remove the entire shield before we could even begin troubleshooting.

We removed the shield, piece by piece, unscrewing many, many screws. The left and right metal sides gave us the most trouble. The left side supports the analog controls. Before we could remove the left side of the shield, we had to first unplug the controls from the main board. Then we had to dislodge the controls from the shield and plug them back into the PC board. Keep in mind, we eventually had to turn on the monitor to test it. So, all the parts had to be connected.

We had the same problem with the right side shield, this time with the power switch. We unplugged the switch from the power supply, removed them from the metal shield and plugged it back into the supply.

Once we had the shield removed completely, we realized that there was no support for the picture tube. We certainly did not want to break off the neck of the CRT while trying to repair the horizontal control. To overcome this obstacle, we fashioned two metal supports for the right and left sides of the monitor and screwed them into place.

To sum up, we completely removed the shield, disconnecting the external controls and power supply as needed. Then, we reconnected all the parts, making sure the controls and switch did not touch any components or heatsinks on the printed circuit boards. Then, we rested the monitor on the metal supports. Now, we were ready to begin troubleshooting.

With everything in order, we plugged the signal cable of the monitor into our test generator and powered up the monitor. In the Magnavox, the horizontal width circuitry is an active circuit. In other words, it contains transistors, diodes, resistors, capacitors, and controls. This is purposely done, so that when the monitor has to adjust for different graphics modes, the circuit can do it automatically.

Rather than trying to troubleshoot blindly, we ordered the service manual from North American Philips (NAP) in Jefferson City, TN. This manual contains a very good schematic diagram. After perusing the diagram for a few minutes, we located the circuitry for the horizontal width control, which is an internal control on this monitor,

We could see from the diagram (see **Figure B.1**) that the horizontal width output transistor was 7512. We measured the voltages around the transistor (base, emitter,

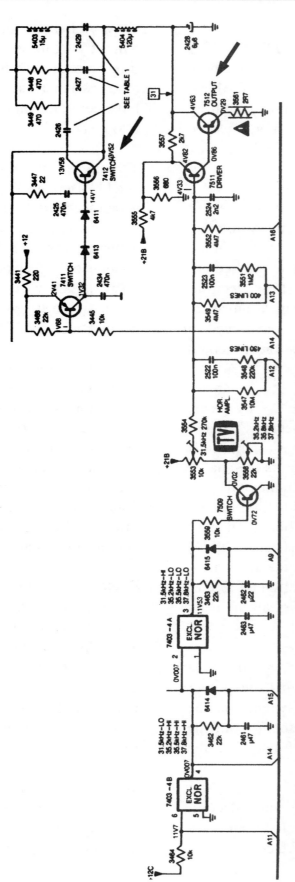

Figure B.1. Schematic diagram of the horizontal width control in the Magnavox 6CM320974I monitor.

and collector) and found that the collector measured 0.24 volts, much lower than expected. This voltage originates at diodes 5408, 5409, and 5410. Thus, we suspected either the diodes or the transistor was bad. We checked the diodes with our DMM set to the diode setting. All of them measured good. We could not reliably check transistor 7512 because it is a Darlington transistor. We found this out by cross referencing the part number, 4822 130 60784, with the ECG book. The ECG number is 261. Just looking at the schematic diagram might lead you to believe that this is a standard NPN transistor; this is not the case.

Since the diodes were good, we desoldered transistor 7512 from the circuit. When we measured the voltage now, it was slightly higher than normal, around 22 volts. This indicated that the transistor was most likely at fault. So we ordered a new one from an authorized NAP dealer, Fox International Ltd., Inc. (Bedford Heights, OH).

We installed the new transistor, making sure the pins (B,C,E) were oriented properly in the holes on the PC board. We measured the voltage at the collector of the transistor; surprisingly, it was still approximately 22 volts. The display, though, was now scanning normally. We tried to adjust the horizontal width control, which is a small potentiometer on the side of the main PC board. Turning the control did not affect the display. We also noticed that the pincushion control was not working.

We made some more measurements. We noticed that turning the horizontal width control had no effect on the base voltage at transistor 7512. This made sense, since

the image on the screen wasn't changing. We had to figure out why we could not vary this voltage.

Frustrated at this point, we decided to examine the PC board from the component side, looking for anything that would give us a clue to the problem. We were looking for broken wires, components touching each other, burned resistors, exploded capacitors, and so forth. We immediately noticed a resistor with a dark burn mark, 3557, a 2.7 kilohm resistor. We had a replacement on hand, so we desoldered and removed the burned resistor and soldered in the new one. Unfortunately, nothing changed. We examined the board again and found another resistor with a slight burn mark, 3441, a 220 ohm 1/2 watt resistor. We replaced this, too. Still, the controls did not work. We looked for more burned resistors, but didn't see any—or any other obvious problems for that matter.

Then, we remembered something—a basic rule. Any time you change a shorted output transistor, you have to replace the emitter resistor, too. This resistor is always destroyed when the output transistor shorts out. Sure enough, when we checked the emitter resistor of transistor 7512, 3561, a 2.7 ohm resistor. It was open.

We found a replacement resistor in our junkbox and soldered it in. Finally, the controls began to work. We were able to adjust the horizontal width and pincushion controls. Using the pattern generator set to the crosshatch pattern, we were able to adjust the display until it looked perfect. We finished up the repair by reassembling the monitor.

We found this repair to be more difficult than it should have been simply because of the way the monitor is constructed. As you might imagine, anything can go wrong when the monitor is not supported by its own chassis. You have to be very careful throughout the repair. Accidentally touch-ing parts together can blow out any num-ber of components. Fortunately, this type of monitor construction is the exception rather than the rule when repairing moni-tors. **Figures B.2** through **B.20** show how this repair was done.

Step-by-Step
Procedure...

Figure B.2. The cross-hatch pattern indicates that the Magavox monitor is over scanning. Adjusting the horizontal width control did not affect the picture at all.

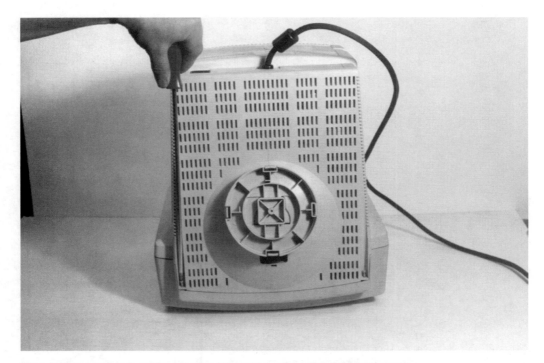

Figure B.3. Removing the screws from the rear cover of the monitor.

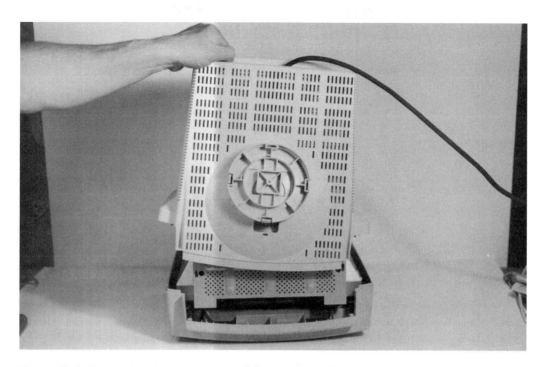

Figure B. 4. Removing the rear cover of the monitor. Notice the monitor can be placed on its face, if it is convenient.

Figure B.5. Using a power screwdriver to remove screws from the monitor's metal shield.

Figure B.6. Removing the rear shield from the monitor.

Figure B.7. Removing the video board from the rear shield.

Figure B.8. Unscrewing the side metal shield from the front of the monitor.

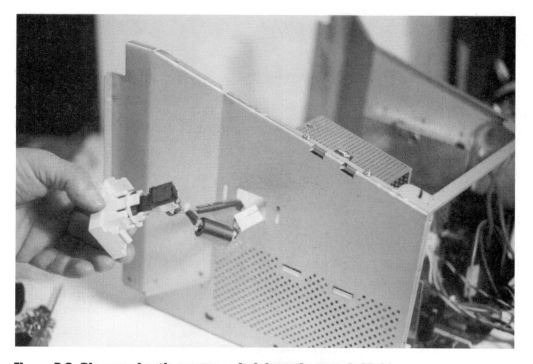

Figure B.9. Disengaging the power switch from the metal shield.

Figure B.10. Removing the shield that surrounds the power switch.

Figure B.11. Disengaging the monitor's external controls from the metal shield.

Figure B.12. Sliding out the main PC board from the bottom shield of the monitor.

Figure B.13. We screwed metal rods to the sides of the monitor for support.

Figure B.14. The metal rods support the monitor when in the upright position.

Figure B.15. The voltage at the collector of the horizontal width output transistor 7512 was 0.24 volts, much lower than expected.

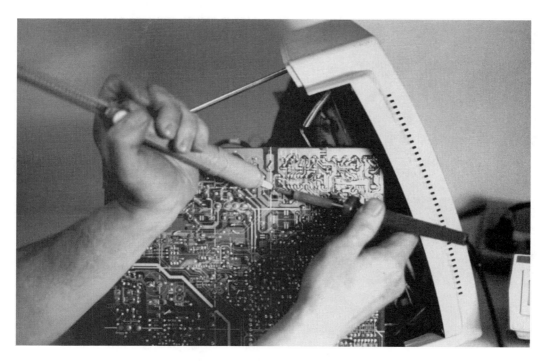

Figure B.16. Desoldering transistor 7512 from the main PC board.

Figure B.17. With the transistor out of the circuit, the voltage jumped to 21.3 volts.

Figure B.18. A close examination of the main PC board revealed a burned resistor.
We replaced this resistor, but the circuit still did not work.

Figure B.19. We decided to remove the emitter resistor for transistor 7512 and
measure it. The measurement showed the resistor was open. Replacing this
resistor solved the problem.

Figure B.20. The display on the Magnavox monitor is now scanning normally.

Appendix C

Case Study 3: AOC Model 4N

Our third case study concerns an AOC Model 4N SVGA monitor. At first we thought we had a dead monitor on our hands. When we plugged it in, nothing happened. But, this monitor has an unusual feature. It will not turn on unless a video signal is supplied to it. So, we connected the monitor to our pattern generator, and turned on the monitor.

At first, a color pattern from the generator appeared on the display. The pattern slowly faded until we could see just a white screen with retrace lines, but no color bars. We attempted to adjust the brightness control, but it had no effect.

We turned off the monitor and removed the cover, which entailed removing three screws and two plastic latches. We turned the monitor on its face to examine the foil side of the main printed circuit board. To be able to view the entire board and especially the area near the controls, we unlatched two plastic rails that held the PC board in place in the cabinet. Then we pulled the board out. Now, we had a perfect view of the controls. With our DMM set to the 200 volts DC setting, we measured the voltage at the center of the brightness control. This is done by placing the negative lead on a ground point and the positive lead on the center pin of the brightness control.

You should be aware that a monitor has two grounds, one hot and one cold. Normally, when you make measurements, you should use the ground that is near the spot where you are measuring. This assures you will be using the right ground. In this case,

the ground was a wide trace near the brightness control.

The voltage at the center pin of the brightness control was really low, approximately 10 volts. It should have been at least 50 or 60 volts. You don't need the service manual to know this. The brightness control goes to the first grid of the picture tube socket. This is clearly marked on the printed circuit board on the neck of the picture tube as G1. The brightness of the picture increases as you lower the voltage of G1. Normally, this voltage is about 35 volts. If the picture is dark, the voltage is about 45 volts. When the picture is bright, the voltage is about 25 volts.

As we turned the brightness control, the voltage at the center of the control stayed the same, 10 volts. A defective potentiometer can cause this, so we tested the control with the DMM set to the ohmmeter setting. As we turned the control, the resistance changed. This indicated that the control was good. This measurement is made by placing one lead of the DMM on the center pin and the other lead on one of the other pins. You must check that both outside pins are working.

Once we were satisfied that the control was okay, we needed to figure out where the outside pin of the brightness control was connected. We followed the traces on the PC board and found that one pin of the control went to ground through a transistor. The other pin usually goes to the power supply. We followed the trace on the printed circuit board until we came to a small resistor, R716 (silkscreened on the board). We turned over the monitor to view the component side of the PC board and saw from the color code on the resistor that R716 was a 220 kilohm resistor.

The voltage on one side of the resistor was about 140 volts coming from the power supply. On the other side of the resistor, the voltage was 10 volts. This indicated that the resistor was open; the voltage should have been at least 50 or 60 volts. We desoldered one lead of the resistor from the printed circuit board and measured the resistance. Sure enough, it was open.

Normally, you would expect zero volts on one side of an open resistor. Why did we measure 10 volts? When a resistor burns, the value of the resistor increases dramatically, simulating an open circuit. But, some voltage still gets through, depending on the load on the other side of the resistor.

We soldered in a new 220 kilohm, 1/2 watt resistor, on the same leads as the old one. The old resistor was 220 kilohms, 1/8 watt. We added a higher wattage resistor to avoid future problems. We soldered the new resistor to the foil side of the PC board. The original resistor was too difficult to get at. Since it was open, it would not affect the resultant resistance.

Now, when we turned on the monitor, the color bar pattern looked very good. Obviously, the brightness control was working normally. We finished up the repair by adjusting the focus to obtain maximum sharpness. The focus adjustment is the top control on the flyback transformer. This adjustment should always be made before reassembling the unit. **Figures C.1** through **C.7** show how this repair was done.

Step-by-Step
Procedure...

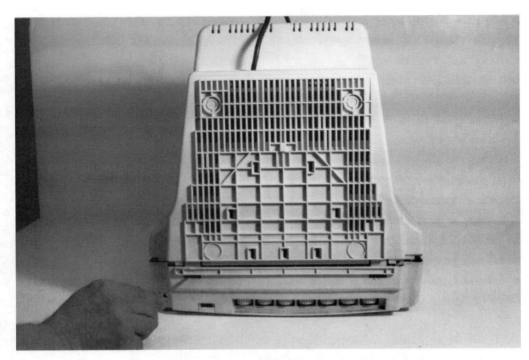

Figure C.1. Pushing in a plastic latch to remove the rear cover of the AOC monitor.

Figure C.2. Pulling out the main PC board to get at the front panel controls.

Figure C.3. The voltage at the center of the brightness control was very low, 10.3 volts DC.

Figure C.4. The defective resistor.

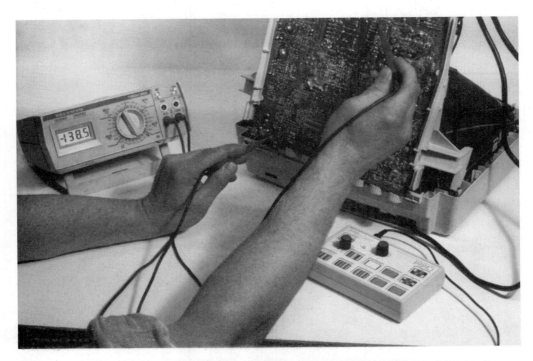

Figure C.5. The voltage on the side of the resistor coming from the power supply measured 138.5 volts DC.

Figure C.6. We soldered the replacement resistor to the foil side of the PC board.

Figure C.7. With the new resistor in place, the brightness of the AOC monitor returned to normal.

Case Study 4:
Magnavox TY15

Our fourth case study concerns a Magnavox Model TY15 composite video monitor. This type of analog monitor was popular years ago with Apple II+ and similar computers. Today, these monitors are useful for video games, security, and VCR hookups. This monitor's color could not be adjusted.

We connected the monitor to a composite video source (an Hitachi VCR). The picture reception was fine but the tint was very pink. We could not adjust the color no matter how much we turned the tint control.

We removed the rear cover of the monitor. The power supply in this monitor is a separate unit that can be released by pressing a plastic latch. We did this and took out the supply. We needed to remove the main circuit board, but this was not easy to do. First, we grounded the anode and removed the anode cap. Next, we removed the CRT board from the CRT. Then, we pulled out the main circuit board to take a look at the front panel controls. We could see that the back of the tint control was cracked.

To fix the problem, we first had to remove a shield that completely covered the foil side of the main PC board. We had to desolder this shield in six places in order to remove it. Once we got the shield off, we desoldered the tint control. We replaced it with a similar part, a 10 kilohm potentiometer, which we found in our junkbox.

The original control had a long plastic shaft. We were lucky to find a replacement part that also had a long shaft. These controls are readily available from parts suppliers, but usually have short shafts. If you couldn't obtain a replacement part with a long shaft, you would either have to extend the shaft in some way or else make do with the short shaft.

We reassembled the monitor by reinstalling the shield and placing the main board into the cabinet. This gave us some trouble, but we finally got the board to seat properly. When we powered up the monitor and tried the tint control, it worked perfectly. **Figures D.1** to **D.9** show how the repair was done.

Step-by-Step Procedure...

Figure D.1. The Magnavox TY15 composite video monitor had fine reception but no color.

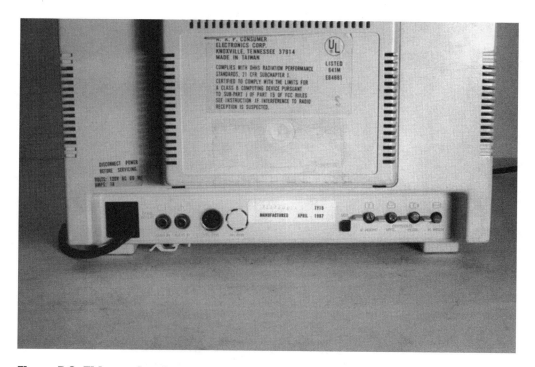

Figure D.2. This monitor has a composite video input, which is the leftmost (RCA jack) input.

Figure D.3. Removing the power supply from the monitor.

Figure D.4. After grounding the anode, we removed the anode cap.

Figure D.5. Removing the CRT board from neck of the picture tube.

Figure D.6. Pulling out the main PC board from the monitor.

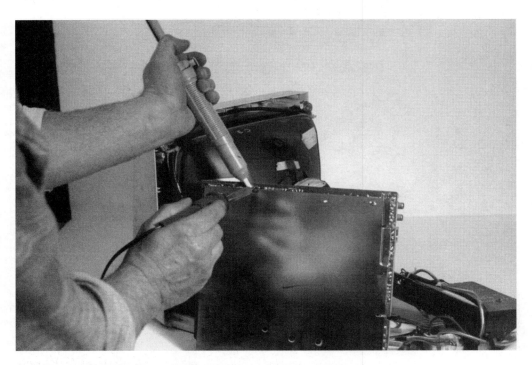

Figure D.7. Desoldering a metal shield from the main PC board.

Figure D.8. The defective tint control removed from the PC board.

Figure D.9. Soldering the new control in place.

Case Study 5:
Magnavox Model 6CM3209741

Our fifth case study concerns another Magnavox Model 6CM320974I monitor. If you have a contract to repair monitors for a company, you will find yourself repairing the same model monitor. Like anything else, companies purchase their computer equipment in bulk. This works in your favor, since you get to know the monitor and will have the service manual on hand after the first repair. The particular problem described here also occurred in the NEC Multisync 4D monitor highlighted throughout the book.

The monitor had a particularly dim display. Turning the brightness control at the front of the monitor had no effect.

We removed the rear cover of the monitor and tried to raise the brightness by adjusting the screen control on the flyback transformer. This had very little effect on the display. It appeared to us as though the cathodes in the CRT needed a cleaning. We decided to check the picture tube with our B&K CRT Tester and Restorer Model 467.

Before we could do this, however, we needed to remove some of the metal shielding surrounding the monitor. We removed the screws from the rear shield and pulled it out about a inch. Then, we removed the top shield. Now, we had just enough room to remove the CRT board from the neck of the picture tube socket.

The B&K CRT Tester usually connects to the picture tube through a socket provided by B&K. Actually, B&K includes five different picture tube sockets with the tester. Unfortunately, none fit the picture tube of the Magnavox monitor.

We solved this dilemma by creating our own picture tube socket. We removed a socket from an old monitor chassis we had on hand and soldered seven wires to it. We attached these wires to one of the sockets supplied with the tester. We used the Magnavox service manual to correctly match the pinouts of the two sockets. The pinouts for the Magnavox picture tube socket are also marked on the small printed circuit board at the neck of the tube. The markings are as follows: KG (cathode green), KB (cathode blue), G2 (screen), G1 (first grid), and HH (filament or heater).

After connecting our homemade socket to the CRT, we turned the main dial of the instrument to SETUP. We adjusted the filament voltage to be exactly 6.3 volts using the left dial (SET HTR). There are three meters at the top. When the main dial is in the SETUP position, the left meter is for the filament, the center meter is for G1, and the right is for the AC line voltage. We set G1 to 50 volts using the SET G1 dial.

Next, we turned the main dial to SET CUT-OFF. In this position, we adjusted the screen voltage for each of the three guns in the picture tube. To do this we adjusted the three dials immediately below the RED, GREEN and BLUE buttons one notch to the right.

When all three of the meters were equal, we switched the main dial to the TEST position. The meters indicate the strength of each of the three guns in the picture tube. If the needle of the meter goes to the green part of the meter face (GOOD), and there is no more than a 10% difference between the three meters, the picture tube is acceptable. In this case, the green was GOOD, but the blue and the red guns were in the red (BAD) area.

Next, we turned the main dial to the RE-STORE position. Then, we pushed the button under each of the three meters for a short time. This instrument applies voltages over the cathode to clean the oxide that accumulates over the years (and prevents electrons from being released from the cathode). The voltage strips a layer of oxide from the cathode so it can again release electrons. This process is called rejuvenation.

We made several attempts at restoring the blue and red guns. Finally, the needles for each meter moved into the GOOD section. We removed the makeshift socket from the picture tube and replaced it with the original. Now, when we turned on the monitor, normal brightness had returned to the picture.

The next step is to adjust the colors. First, we turned off all the colors until we got a black and white background. We used a pattern generator set to a black and white crosshatch pattern. We adjusted the black and white picture until it looked good and then gave it a little bit of a blue tint from the controls on the picture tube socket. We finished up by turning on the color. The picture now looked perfect.

We were fortunate in this case. Sometimes, when you give a gun a short burst, the whole picture tube goes dead. So, if you are doing this procedure for a customer, you have to warn him or her that the monitor may be ruined completely. But, at this point in the life of the monitor, you have little choice. A new picture tube could cost more than the monitor is worth. **Figures E.1** to **E.11** show how the repair was done.

Step-by-Step Procedure...

Figure E.1. Unscrewing the rear shield of the monitor.

Figure E.2. Pulling the rear shield out a couple of inches to get at the CRT board.

Figure E.3. Removing the top shield of the monitor.

Figure E.4. With just enough room to maneuver, we removed the CRT board from the neck of the CRT.

Figure E.5. Preparing to connect a socket to the neck of the picture tube. Note that we wired this socket to the socket that comes with the CRT tester.

Figure E.6. The socket is connected to the picture tube.

Figure E.7. The B&K CRT Tester in the SET CUTOFF mode.

Figure E.8. With the B&K Tester/Restorer in the RESTORE position, we pushed the button to restore the red cathode.

Figure E.9. After restoring all three cathodes, the needles on the meters moved into the GOOD section.

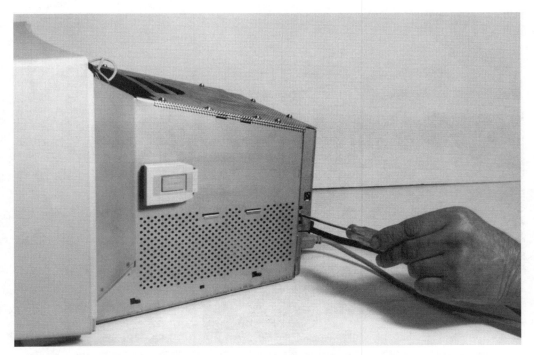

Figure E.10. We finished up the repair by adjusting the color controls on the video board.

Figure E.11. After restoring the CRT, the picture on the Magnavox monitor was back to normal.

Case Study 6:
NEC VGA APCH5300

Our sixth case study concerns a NEC Enhanced VGA Color Display APCH530 monitor. This monitor had a poorly focused image. We verified the problem by running a test pattern over the screen consisting of rows of the number 4 running from top to bottom. We could see that the monitor needed a focus adjustment.

We removed the rear cover of the monitor and located the focus adjustment on the body of the flyback transformer. We reached this control by placing a Phillips head screwdriver through a cutout in a metal shield on the side of the monitor. The top control of the flyback is for the focus, the bottom control is for the screen voltage.

We slowly turned the control to the left and to the right. As we did this, we watched the screen go from blurry to sharp and back to blurry again. We adjusted the control until the display looked sharpest, which was quite acceptable. We left the focus adjustment in that position and re-assembled the monitor. This completed the repair.

With a repair like this one, which is simply an adjustment of the focus control, the source of the problem may lie with the flyback transformer. This must be explained to the customer. Otherwise, you may wind up in a situation where the customer is demanding that you fix the monitor for free the next time it goes out of focus. **Figures F.1** to **F.6** show how the repair was done.

Step-by-Step Procedure...

Figure F.1. Before adjusting the focus, we selected a pattern from The Troubleshooter software that filled the screen with 4's.

Figure F.2. Unscrewing the rear cover of the monitor.

Figure F.3. Removing a screw at the bottom of the monitor.

Figure F.4. Removing the rear cover. Note that for this NEC monitor, the tilt and swivel stand does not connect to the rear cover.

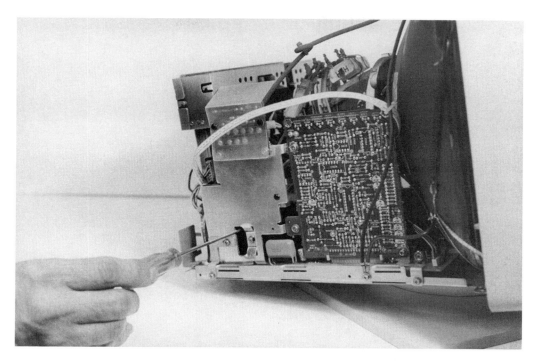

Figure F.5. Adjusting the focus control on the flyback through the metal shield.

Figure F.6. The focus is now greatly improved.

Appendix G
Company Listings

Chemtronics, Inc.
8125 Cobb Center Dr.
Kennesaw, GA 30152
Tel.: 1-800-645-5244; Fax: 770-423-0748

Computer and Monitor Maintenance, Inc.
6649-N1 Peachtree Ind. Blvd.
Norcross, GA 30092
Tel.: 770-662-5633; Fax: 770-840-8814

Dalbani
4225 NW 72nd Ave.
Miami, FL 33166
Tel.: 1-800-325-2264; Fax: 305-594-6588

East Coast Transistor
PO Box 238
West Hempstead, NY 11552
Tel.: 1-800-645-3516; Fax: 516-483-5904

Electro Dynamics Inc. (EDI)
P.O. Box 9022, 135 Eileen Way
Syosset, NY 11791-9022
Tel.: 1-800-426-6423; Fax: 1-800-873-2948

ForeFront
25400 U.S. Highway 19 N.
Suite 285
Clearwater, FL 34623
Tel.: 1-800-475-5831; Fax: 813-726-6922

Howard W. Sams & Company
2647 Waterfront Parkway, E. Dr., Ste. 100
Indianapolis, IN 46214
Tel.: 800-428-7267; Fax: 317-298-5604

International Components Marketing
1545 Sawtelle Blvd., Suite 21
Los Angeles, CA 90025
Tel.: 800-748-6232; Fax: 310-445-5003

Jensen Tools, Inc.
7815 S. 46th St.
Phoenix, AZ 85044
Tel.: 800-366-9662; Fax: 602-438-1690

MAT Electronics
400 Pike Rd.
Huntington Valley, PA 19006-1610
Tel.: 1-800-628-1118; Fax: 1-800-628-1005

Parts Express
340 E. First St.
Dayton, OH 45402-1257
Tel.: 1-800-338-0531; Fax: 937-222-4644

Philips Consumer Electronics Co.
Technical Publications Dept.
P.O. Box 177, Old Andrew Johnson Hwy.
Jefferson City, TN 37760
Tel.: 800-851-8885; Fax: 800-535-3715

Philips ECG
1025 Westminster Dr.
Williamsport, PA 17701

RNJ Electronics, Inc.
202 New Highway
P.O. Box 667
Amityville, NY 11701-0667
Tel.: 1-800-645-5833; Fax: 516-226-2770

Sencore

3200 Sencore Dr.

Sioux Falls, SD 57107

Tel.: 1-800-SENCORE; Fax: 605-339-0317

Sonera Technologies

P.O. Box 565

Rumson, NJ 07760

Tel.: 908-747-6886; Fax: 908-747-4523

Suburban Electronic Wholesalers

4905 Suitland Rd.

Suitland, MD 20746

Tel.: 1-800-341-5353; Fax: 1-800-341-5354

Techni-Tool

5 Apollo Rd., Box 368

Plymouth Meeting, PA 19462

Tel.: 610-941-2400; Fax: 610-828-5623

Appendix H
VESA Video Models

VESA standards for various video modes.

VGA 640 x 480	f_H (KHz) 37.861 f_V (Hz) 72.809
800/56Hz 800 x 600	f_H (KHz) 35.156 f_V (Hz) 56.250
800/72Hz 800 x 600	f_H (KHz) 48.077 f_V (Hz) 72.188
1024/60Hz 1024 x 768	f_H (KHz) 48.363 f_V (Hz) 60.004
1024/70Hz 1024 x 768	f_H (KHz) 56.476 f_V (Hz) 70.069
1280/60Hz 1280 x 1024	f_H (KHz) 63.702 f_V (Hz) 60.096
MAC/832/75Hz 832 x 624	f_H (KHz) 49.726 f_V (Hz) 74.551

f_H is the horizontal sync frequency and f_V is the vertical sync frequency.

Index

The Howard W. Sams
Troubleshooting & Repair Guide to TV
Howard W. Sams & Company

The Howard W. Sams Troubleshooting & Repair Guide to TV is the most complete and up-to-date television repair book available. Included in its more than 300 pages is complete repair information for all makes of TVs, time-saving features that even the pros don't know, comprehensive basic electronics information, and extensive coverage of common TV symptoms.

This repair guide is completely illustrated with useful photos, schematics, graphs, and flowcharts. It covers audio, video, technician safety, test equipment, power supplies, picture-in-picture, and much more. *The Howard W. Sams Troubleshooting & Repair Guide to TV* was written, illustrated, and assembled by the engineers and technicians of Howard W. Sams & Company. This book is the first truly comprehensive television repair guide published in the 90s, and it contains vast amounts of information never printed in book form before.

Video Technology
384 pages Paperback ◆ 8-1/2 x 11"
ISBN: 0-7906-1077-9 ◆ Sams: 61077
$29.95 ($39.95 Canada) ◆ June 1996

TV Video
Systems
L.W. Pena & Brent A. Pena

Knowing which video programming source to choose, and knowing what to do with it once you have it, can seem overwhelming. Covering standard hard-wired cable, large-dish satellite systems, and DSS, *TV Video Systems* explains the different systems, how they are installed, their advantages and disadvantages, and how to troubleshoot problems. This book presents easy-to-understand information and illustrations covering installation instructions, home options, apartment options, detecting and repairing problems, and more. The in-depth chapters guide you through your TV video project to a successful conclusion.

L.W. Pena is an independent certified cable TV technician with 14 years of experience who has installed thousands of TV video systems in homes and businesses. Brent Pena has eight years of experience in computer science and telecommunications, with additional experience as a cable installer.

Video Technology
124 pages ◆ Paperback ◆ 6 x 9"
ISBN: 0-7906-1082-5 ◆ Sams: 61082
$14.95 ($20.95 Canada) ◆ June 1996

ES&T Presents TV Troubleshooting & Repair
Electronic Servicing & Technology Magazine

TV set servicing has never been easy. The service manager, service technician, and electronics hobbyist need timely, insightful information in order to locate the correct service literature, make a quick diagnosis, obtain the correct replacement components, complete the repair, and get the TV back to the owner.

ES&T Presents TV Troubleshooting & Repair presents information that will make it possible for technicians and electronics hobbyists to service TVs faster, more efficiently, and more economically, thus making it more likely that customers will choose not to discard their faulty products, but to have them restored to service by a trained, competent professional.

Originally published in *Electronic Servicing & Technology*, the chapters in this book are articles written by professional technicians, most of whom service TV sets every day. These chapters provide general descriptions of television circuit operation, detailed service procedures, and diagnostic hints.

Video Technology
226 pages ◆ Paperback ◆ 6 x 9"
ISBN: 0-7906-1086-8 ◆ Sams: 61086
$18.95 ($25.95 Canada) ◆ August 1996

CALL 1-800-428-7267 TODAY FOR THE NAME OF
YOUR NEAREST PROMPT PUBLICATIONS DISTRIBUTOR

Theory & Design of Loudspeaker Enclosures
Dr. J. Ernest Benson

The design of loudspeaker enclosures, particularly vented enclosures, has been a subject of continuing interest since 1930. Since that time, a wide range of interests surrounding loudspeaker enclosures have sprung up that grapple with the various aspects of the subject, especially design. *Theory & Design of Loudspeaker Enclosures* lays the groundwork for readers who want to understand the general functions of loudspeaker enclosure systems and eventually experiment with their own design.

Written for design engineers and technicians, students and intermediate-to-advanced level acoustics enthusiasts, this book presents a general theory of loudspeaker enclosure systems. Full of illustrated and numerical examples, this book examines diverse developments in enclosure design, and studies the various types of enclosures as well as varying parameter values and performance optimization.

Audio Technology
244 pages ◆ Paperback ◆ 6 x 9"
ISBN: 0-7906-1093-0 ◆ Sams: 61093
$19.95 ($26.99 Canada) ◆ August 1996

The In-Home VCR Mechanical Repair & Cleaning Guide
Curt Reeder

Like any machine that is used i the home or office, a VCR requires min mal service to keep it functioning we and for a long time. However, a tech nical or electrical engineering degre is not required to begin regular mair tenance on a VCR. This book show readers the tricks and secrets of VC maintenance using just a few sma hand tools, such as tweezers and power screwdriver.

This book is also geared toward entrepreneurs who ma consider starting a new VCR service business of their own.

Video Technology
222 pages ◆ Paperback ◆ 8-3/8 x 10-7/8"
ISBN: 0-7906-1076-0 ◆ Sams: 61076
$19.95 ($26.99 Canada) ◆ April 1996

The Video Book
Gordon McComb

Televisions and video cassette recorders have become part of everyday life, but few people know how to get the mos out of these home entertainment devices. *The Video Book* offers easy-to-read text and clearly illustrated examples t guide readers through the use, installation, connection, and care of video system components. Simple enough for the ne buyer, yet detailed enough to assure proper connection of the units after purchase, this book is a necessary addition to th library of every modern video consumer. Topics included in the coverage are the operating basics of TVs, VCRs, satelli systems, and video cameras; maintenance and troubleshooting; and connectors, cables, and system interconnections.

Gordon McComb has written over 35 books and 1,000 magazine articles, which have appeared in such publications *Popular Science*, *Video*, *PC World*, and *Omni*, as well as many other top consumer and trade publications. His writing ha spanned a wide range of subjects, from computers to video to robots.

Video Technology
192 pages ◆ Paperback ◆ 6 x 9"
ISBN: 0-7906-1030-2 ◆ Sams: 61030
$16.95 ($22.99 Canada) ◆ October 1992

**CALL 1-800-428-7267 TODAY FOR THE NAME OF
YOUR NEAREST PROMPT PUBLICATIONS DISTRIBUTOR**

Is This Thing On?
Gordon McComb

Is This Thing On? takes readers through each step of selecting components, installing, adjusting, and maintaining a sound system for small meeting rooms, churches, lecture halls, public-address systems for schools or offices, or any other large room.

In easy-to-understand terms, drawings and illustrations, Is This Thing On? explains the exact procedures behind connections and troubleshooting diagnostics. With the help of this book, hobbyists and technicians can avoid problems that often occur while setting up sound systems for events and lectures.

Is This Thing On? covers basic components of sound systems, the science of acoustics, enclosed room, sound system specifications, wiring sound systems, and how to install wireless microphones, CD players, portable public-address systems, and more.

Audio Technology
136 pages ◆ Paperback ◆ 6 x 9"
ISBN: 0-7906-1081-7 ◆ Sams: 61081
$14.95 ($20.95 Canada) ◆ April 1996

Advanced Speaker Designs
Ray Alden

Advanced Speaker Designs shows the hobbyist and the experienced technician how to create high-quality speaker systems for the home, office, or auditorium. Every part of the system is covered in detail, from the driver and crossover network to the enclosure itself. Readers can build speaker systems from the parts lists and instructions provided, or they can actually learn to calculate design parameters, system responses, and component values with scientific calculators or PC software.

This book includes construction plans for seven complete systems, easy-to-understand instructions and illustrations, and chapters on sealed and vented enclosures. There is also emphasis placed on enhanced bass response, computer-aided speaker design, and driver parameters. Advanced Speaker Designs is a companion book to Speakers for Your Home and Automobile, also available from Prompt® Publications.

Audio Technology
136 pages ◆ Paperback ◆ 6 x 9"
ISBN: 0-7906-1070-1 ◆ Sams: 61070
$16.95 ($22.99 Canada) ◆ July 1995

Making Sense of Sound
Alvis J. Evans

This book deals with the subject of sound — how it is detected and processed using electronics in equipment that spans the full spectrum of consumer electronics. It concentrates on explaining basic concepts and fundamentals to provide easy-to-understand information, yet it contains enough detail to be of high interest to the serious practitioner. Discussion begins with how sound propagates and common sound characteristics, before moving on to the more advanced concepts of amplification and distortion. Making Sense of Sound was designed to cover a broad scope, yet in enough detail to be a useful reference for readers at every level.

Alvis Evans is the author of many books on the subject of electricity and electronics for beginning hobbyists and advanced technicians. He teaches seminars and workshops worldwide to members of the trade, as well as being an Associate Professor of Electronics at Tarrant County Junior College.

Audio Technology
112 pages ◆ Paperback ◆ 6 x 9"
ISBN: 0-7906-1026-4 ◆ Sams: 61026
$10.95 ($14.95 Canada) ◆ November 1992

CALL 1-800-428-7267 TODAY FOR THE NAME OF
YOUR NEAREST PROMPT PUBLICATIONS DISTRIBUTOR

▼ ▼ ▼ ▼ ▼ ▼ ▼ ▼ ▼ ▼ ▼ ▼ ▼ ▼

Semiconductor Cross Reference Book
Fourth Edition
Howard W. Sams & Company

This newly revised and updated reference book is the most comprehensive guide to replacement data available for engineers, technicians, and those who work with semiconductors. With more than 490,000 part numbers, type numbers, and other identifying numbers listed, technicians will have no problem locating the replacement or substitution information needed. There is not another book on the market that can rival the breadth and reliability of information available in the fourth edition of the *Semiconductor Cross Reference Book*.

Professional Reference
688 pages ◆ Paperback ◆ 8-1/2 x 11"
ISBN: 0-7906-1080-9 ◆ Sams: 61080
$24.95 ($33.95 Canada) ◆ August 1996

The Component Identifier
and Source Book
Victor Meeldijk

Because interface designs are often r verse engineered using component data block diagrams that list only part numbe technicians are often forced to search f replacement parts armed only with man facturer logos and part numbers.

This source book was written to ass technicians and system designers in iden fying components from prefixes and logo as well as find sources for various types microcircuits and other components. The is not another book on the market that lists as many manufacturers such diverse electronic components.

Professional Reference
384 pages ◆ Paperback ◆ 8-1/2 x 11"
ISBN: 0-7906-1088-4 ◆ Sams: 61088
$24.95 ($33.95 Canada) ◆ November 1996

IC Cross Reference Book
Second Edition
Howard W. Sams & Company

The engineering staff of Howard W. Sams & Company assembled the *IC Cross Reference Book* to help readers find replacements or substitutions for more than 35,000 ICs and modules. It is an easy-to-use cross reference guide and includes part numbers for the United States, Europe, and the Far East. This reference book was compiled from manufacturers' data and from the analysis of consumer electronics devices for PHOTOFACT® service data, which has been relied upon since 1946 by service technicians worldwide.

Professional Reference
192 pages ◆ Paperback ◆ 8-1/2 x 11"
ISBN: 0-7906-1096-5 ◆ Sams: 61096
$19.95 ($26.99 Canada) ◆ November 1996

Tube Substitution
Handbook
William Smith & Barry Buchanan

The most accurate, up-to-date guid available, the *Tube Substitution Handbook* useful to antique radio buffs, old car enth siasts, and collectors of vintage ham rad equipment. In addition, marine operato microwave repair technicians, and TV ar radio technicians will find the *Handbook* be an invaluable reference tool.

The *Tube Substitution Handbook* is divid into three sections, each preceded by sp cific instructions. These sections are vacuu tubes, picture tubes, and tube basing diagrams.

Professional Reference
149 pages ◆ Paperback ◆ 6 x 9"
ISBN: 0-7906-1036-1 ◆ Sams: 61036
$16.95 ($22.99 Canada) ◆ March 1995

CALL 1-800-428-7267 TODAY FOR THE NAME OF
YOUR NEAREST PROMPT PUBLICATIONS DISTRIBUTOR

PROMPT®
PUBLICATIONS

Alternative Energy

Mark E. Hazen

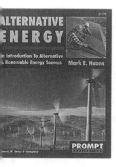

This book is designed to introduce readers to the many different forms of energy mankind has learned to put to use. Generally, energy sources are harnessed for the purpose of producing electricity. This process relies on transducers to transform energy from one form into another. *Alternative Energy* will not only address transducers and the five most common sources of energy that can be converted to electricity, it will also explore solar energy, the harnessing of the wind for energy, geothermal energy, and nuclear energy.

This book is designed to be an introduction to energy and alternate sources of electricity. Each of the nine chapters are followed by questions to test comprehension, making it ideal for students and teachers alike. In addition, listings of World Wide Web sites are included so that readers can learn more about alternative energy and the organizations devoted to it.

Professional Reference
320 pages ◆ Paperback ◆ 7-3/8 x 9-1/4"
ISBN: 0-7906-1079-5 ◆ Sams: 61079
$18.95 ($25.95 Canada) ◆ October 1996

The Complete RF Technician's Handbook

Cotter W. Sayre

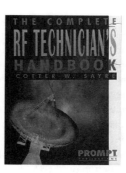

The *Complete RF Technician's Handbook* will furnish the working technician or student with a solid grounding in the latest methods and circuits employed in today's RF communications gear. It will also give readers the ability to test and troubleshoot transmitters, transceivers, and receivers with absolute confidence. Some of the topics covered include reactance, phase angle, logarithms, diodes, passive filters, amplifiers, and distortion. Various multiplexing methods and data, satellite, spread spectrum, cellular, and microwave communication technologies are discussed.

Cotter W. Sayre is an electronics design engineer with Goldstar Development, Inc., in Lake Elsinore, California. He is a graduate of Los Angeles Pierce College and is certified by the National Association of Radio and Telecommunications Engineers, as well as the International Society of Electronics Technicians.

Professional Reference
281 pages ◆ Paperback ◆ 8-1/2 x 11"
ISBN: 0-7906-1085-X ◆ Sams: 61085
$24.95 ($33.95 Canada) ◆ July 1996

Surface-Mount Technology for PC Boards

James K. Hollomon, Jr.

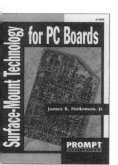

The race to adopt surface-mount technology, or SMT as it is known, has been described as the latest revolution in electronics. This book is intended for the working engineer or manager, the student or the interested layman, who would like to learn to deal effectively with the many trade-offs required to produce high manufacturing yields, low test costs, and manufacturable designs using SMT. The valuable information presented in *Surface-Mount Technology for PC Boards* includes the benefits and limitations of SMT, SMT and FPT components, manufacturing methods, reliability and quality assurance, and practical applications.

James K. Hollomon, Jr. is the founder and president of AMTI, an R&D and prototyping service concentrating on miniaturization and low-noise, high-speed applications. He has nearly 20 years experience in engineering, marketing, and managing firms dealing with leadless components. His previous appointments include national president of the Surface-Mount Technology Association.

Professional Reference
510 pages ◆ Paperback ◆ 7 x 10"
ISBN: 0-7906-1060-4 ◆ Sams: 61060
$26.95 ($36.95 Canada) ◆ July 1995

CALL 1-800-428-7267 TODAY FOR THE NAME OF YOUR NEAREST PROMPT PUBLICATIONS DISTRIBUTOR

▼ ▼ ▼ ▼ ▼ ▼ ▼ ▼ ▼ ▼ ▼

Internet Guide to the Electronics Industry
John Adams

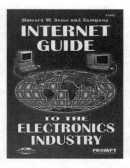

Although the Internet pervades our lives, it would not have been possible without the growth of electronics. It is very fitting then that technical subjects, data sheets, parts houses, and of course manufacturers, are developing new and innovative ways to ride along the Information Superhighway. Whether it's programs that calculate Ohm's Law or a schematic of a satellite system, electronics hobbyists and technicians can find a wealth of knowledge and information on the Internet.

In fact, soon electronics hobbyists and professionals will be able to access on-line catalogs from manufacturers and distributors all over the world, and then order parts, schematics, and other merchandise without leaving home. The *Internet Guide to the Electronics Industry* serves mainly as a directory to the resources available to electronics professionals and hobbyists.

Internet
192 pages ♦ Paperback ♦ 5-1/2 x 8-1/2"
ISBN: 0-7906-1092-2 ♦ Sams: 61092
$16.95 ($22.99 Canada) ♦ December 1996

Real-World Interfacing with Your PC
James "J.J." Barbarello

As the computer becomes increasing prevalent in society, its functions and appcations continue to expand. Modern soft ware allows users to do everything fro balance a checkbook to create a family tre Interfacing, however, is truly the wave the future for those who want to use the computer for things other than manipula ing text, data, and graphics.

Real-World Interfacing With Your PC pr vides all the information necessary to use PC's parallel port as a gateway to electronic interfacing. In addition hardware fundamentals, this book provides a basic understanding how to write software to control hardware.

While the book is geared toward electronics hobbyists, it includes chapter on project design and construction techniques, a checklist fo easy reference, and a recommended inventory of starter electron parts to which readers at every level can relate.

Computer Technology
119 pages ♦ Paperback ♦ 7-3/8 x 9-1/4"
ISBN: 0-7906-1078-7 ♦ Sams: 61078
$16.95 ($22.99 Canada) ♦ March 1996

ES&T Presents Computer Troubleshooting & Repair
Electronic Servicing & Technology

ES&T is the nation's most popular magazine for professionals who service consumer electronics equipment. PROMPT Publications, a rising star in the technical publishing business, is combining its publishing expertise with the experience ar knowledge of *ES&T's* best writers to produce a new line of troubleshooting and repair books for the electronics marke Compiled from articles and prefaced by the editor in chief, Nils Conrad Persson, these books provide valuable, hands-c information for anyone interested in electronics and product repair.

Computer Troubleshooting & Repair is the second book in the series and features information on repairing Macintosh con puters, a CD-ROM primer, and a color monitor. Also included are hard drive troubleshooting and repair tips, comput diagnostic software, networking basics, preventative maintenance for computers, upgrading, and much more.

Computer Technology
288 pages ♦ Paperback ♦ 6 x 9"
ISBN: 0-7906-1087-6 ♦ Sams: 61087
$18.95 ($26.50 Canada) ♦ February 1997

CALL 1-800-428-7267 TODAY FOR THE NAME OF YOUR NEAREST PROMPT PUBLICATIONS DISTRIBUTOR

PROMPT®
PUBLICATIONS

The Phone Book

Gerald Luecke & James Allen

This book is an installation guide for telephones and telephone accessories. It was written to make it easier for the inexperienced person to install telephones, whether existing ones are being replaced or moved or new ones added, without the hassle and expense of contracting a serviceman. *The Phone Book* begins by explaining the telephone system and its operation, before moving onto clear step-by-step instructions for replacing and adding telephones. With this book, a minimum of tools available around the house, and readily available parts, readers will be able to handle any telephone installation in the home, apartment, or small business.

Gerald Luecke has written articles on integrated circuits and digital technology for numerous trade and professional organizations. James Allen is the President, CEO, and a director of Master Publishing.

Communication
176 pages ✦ Paperback ✦ 7-3/8 x 9-1/4”
ISBN: 0-7906-1028-0 ✦ Sams: 61028
$16.95 ($22.99 Canada) ✦ October 1992

Digital Electronics

Stephen Kamichik

Although the field of digital electronics emerged years ago, there has never been a definitive guide to its theories, principles, and practices — until now. *Digital Electronics* is written as a textbook for a first course in digital electronics, but its applications are varied.

Useful as a guide for independent study, the book also serves as a review for practicing technicians and engineers. And because *Digital Electronics* does not assume prior knowledge of the field, the hobbyist can gain insight about digital electronics.

Some of the topics covered include analog circuits, logic gates, flip-flops, and counters. In addition, a problem set appears at the end of each chapter to test the reader's understanding and comprehension of the materials presented. Detailed instructions are provided so that the readers can build the circuits described in this book to verify their operation.

Electronic Theory
150 pages ✦ Paperback ✦ 7-3/8 x 9-1/4”
ISBN: 0-7906-1075-2 ✦ Sams: 61075
$16.95 ($22.99 Canada) ✦ February 1996

The Right Antenna

Alvis J. Evans

The Right Antenna is intended to provide easy-to-understand information on a wide variety of antennas. It begins by explaining how antennas work and then isolates antennas for TV and FM. A separate chapter is devoted to satellite TV antennas, noise and interference, and antennas used by hams for antenna band operation. The basic concepts of cellular telephone system operation are explained and the most popular antennas are discussed. After studying this book, the reader will be able to select an antenna, place it correctly, and install it properly to obtain maximum performance whether in a strong signal area or in a fringe area.

Alvis Evans is the author of many books on the subject of electricity and electronics for beginning hobbyists and advanced technicians. He teaches seminars and workshops worldwide to members of the trade, as well as being an Associate Professor of Electronics at Tarrant County Junior College.

Communication
112 pages ✦ Paperback ✦ 6 x 9”
ISBN: 0-7906-1022-1 ✦ Sams: 61022
$10.95 ($14.95 Canada) ✦ November 1992

CALL 1-800-428-7267 TODAY FOR THE NAME OF YOUR NEAREST PROMPT PUBLICATIONS DISTRIBUTOR

PROMPT
PUBLICATIONS

Semiconductor Essentials

Stephen Kamichik

Readers will gain hands-on knowledge of semiconductor diodes and transistors with help from the information in this book. *Semiconductor Essentials* is a first course in electronics at the technical and engineering levels. Each chapter is a lesson in electronics, with problems included to test understanding of the material presented. This generously illustrated manual is a useful instructional tool for the student and hobbyist, as well as a practical review for professional technicians and engineers. The comprehensive coverage includes semiconductor chemistry, rectifier diodes, zener diodes, transistor biasing, and more.

Author Stephen Kamichik is an electronics consultant who has developed dozens of electronic products and received patents in both the U.S. and Canada. He holds degrees in electrical engineering, and was employed by SPAR, where he worked on the initial prototyping of the Canadarm.

Electronic Theory
112 pages ✦ Paperback ✦ 6 x 9"
ISBN: 0-7906-1071-X ✦ Sams: 61071
$16.95 ($22.99 Canada) ✦ September 1995

Introduction to Microprocessor Theory & Operation

J.A. Sam Wilson & Joseph Risse

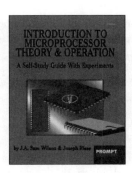

This book takes readers into the hea of computerized equipment and reve how microprocessors work. By coveri digital circuits in addition to microproce sors and providing self-tests and expe ments, *Introduction to Microprocessor Theory Operation* makes it easy to learn micropi cessor systems. The text is fully illustrat with circuits, specifications, and pinouts guide beginners through the ins-and-o of microprocessors, as well as provide e perienced technicians with a valuable reference and refresher tool.

J.A. Sam Wilson has written numerous books covering all aspec of the electronics field, and has served as the Director of Techni Publications for NESDA. Joseph Risse develops courses and labor tory experiments in self-study and industrial electronics for Interr tional Correspondence Schools and other independent study schoo

Electronic Theory
211 pages ✦ Paperback ✦ 6 x 9"
ISBN: 0-7906-1064-7 ✦ Sams: 61064
$16.95 ($22.99 Canada) ✦ February 1995

Basic Principles of Semiconductors

Irving M. Gottlieb

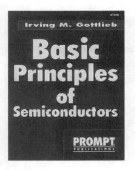

Despite their ever-growing prominence in the electronics industry, semiconductors are still plagued by a stigma whi defines them merely as poor conductors. This narrow-sighted view fails to take into account the fact that semiconductors a truly unique alloys whose conductivity is enhanced tenfold by the addition of even the smallest amount of light, voltage, he or certain other substances. *Basic Principles of Semiconductors* explores the world of semiconductors, beginning with an int duction to atomic physics before moving onto the structure, theory, applications, and future of these still-evolving allo Such a theme makes this book useful to a wide spectrum of practitioners, from the hobbyist and student, right up to t technician and the professional electrician. Irving M. Gottlieb is the author of over ten books in the electrical and electron fields. *Basic Principles of Semiconductors* is his latest offering, however *Test Procedures for Basic Electronics* is also available fr PROMPT® Publications.

Electronic Theory
158 pages ✦ Paperback ✦ 6 x 9"
ISBN: 0-7906-1066-3 ✦ Sams: 61066
$14.95 ($20.95 Canada) ✦ April 1995

CALL 1-800-428-7267 TODAY FOR THE NAME OF
YOUR NEAREST PROMPT PUBLICATIONS DISTRIBUTOR

Managing the Computer Power Environment
Mark Waller

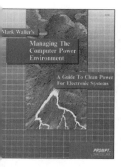

Clean power is what every computer system needs to operate without error. But electricity's voyage from utility company to home or office introduces noise, surges, static, and a host of gremlins that can seriously affect computer performance and data security. Written for data processing specialists, field engineers, technicians, and computer network professionals, *Managing the Computer Power Environment* provides the background in electrical technology that will help readers understand and control the quality of the power that drives their computer system. Covering utility power, grounding, power distribution units, and back-up power systems and conditioners, Mark Waller prepares the reader to manage the demons of electrical destruction through ensuring clean power for your electronic system. Mark Waller is president of the Waller Group, Inc., a company specializing in solving electrical power and grounding problems.

Electrical Technology
174 pages ◆ Paperback ◆ 7-3/8 x 9-1/4"
ISBN: 0-7906-1020-5 ◆ Sams: 61020
$19.95 ($26.99 Canada) ◆ April 1992

Surges, Sags and Spikes
Mark Waller

Surges, sags, spikes, brownouts, blackouts, lightning and other damaging electrical power disturbances can render a personal computer system and its data useless in a few milliseconds — unless you're prepared. Mark Waller's *Surges, Sags and Spikes* is written for all personal computer users concerned with protecting their computer systems against a hostile electrical environment. In easy-to-understand, nontechnical language, the author takes a comprehensive look at approaches to solving computer power problems. Helpful diagrams and photographs are included to document computer power needs and solutions.

Mark Waller is an award-winning author whose numerous articles have appeared in such magazines as *Byte*, *Datamation*, and *Network World*. He is the author of another book dealing with power entitled *Managing the Computer Power Environment*, also available from PROMPT® Publications.

Electrical Technology
220 pages ◆ Paperback ◆ 7-3/8 x 9-1/4"
ISBN: 0-7906-1019-1 ◆ Sams: 61019
$19.95 ($26.99 Canada) ◆ April 1992

Harmonics
Mark Waller

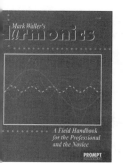

Harmonics is the essential guide to understanding all of the issues and areas of concern surrounding harmonics and the recognized methods for dealing with them. Covering nonlinear loads, multiple PCs, K-factor transformers, and more, Mark Waller prepares the reader to manage problems often encountered in electrical distribution systems that can be solved easily through an understanding of harmonics, current, and voltage. This book is a useful tool for system and building engineers, electricians, maintenance personnel, and all others concerned about protecting and maintaining the quality of electrical power systems.

Mark Waller is president of the Waller Group, Inc., and specializes in harmonic analysis and in solving electrical power and grounding problems for facilities. He has been actively involved in the field of electrical power quality for many years. Waller has a broad background in all aspects of power quality, power protection, and system integrity.

Electrical Technology
132 pages ◆ Paperback ◆ 7-3/8 x 9-1/4"
ISBN: 0-7906-1048-5 ◆ Sams: 61048
$24.95 ($33.95 Canada) ◆ May 1994

CALL 1-800-428-7267 TODAY FOR THE NAME OF
YOUR NEAREST PROMPT PUBLICATIONS DISTRIBUTOR

▼ ▼ ▼ ▼ ▼ ▼ ▼ ▼ ▼ ▼ ▼ ▼

About The Author

Vaughn D. Martin is a senior electrical engineer with the Department of the Air Force. Previously he worked at Magnavox and ITT Aerospace/Optics, where he acquired his fascination with optoelectronics. He has published numerous articles in trade, amateur radio, electronic hobbyist, troubleshooting and repair, and optoelectronics magazines. He has also written several books covering a wide range of topics in the field of electronics.

COMING SUMMER 1997!
Optoelectronics
Volume 3
Vaughn D. Martin

Optoelectronics, Volume 3 is an Advanced self-teaching text that contains:

• Information on Fiber Optics!

• Lab experiments for your own home lab, professional lab, or classroom!

• AND MUCH MORE!

Optoelectronics, Volume 3
400 pages ◆ Paperback ◆ 8-1/2 x 11"
ISBN: PENDING ◆ Sams: PENDING
$29.95 ◆ August 1997

**CALL 1-800-428-7267 TODAY FOR THE NAME OF
YOUR NEAREST PROMPT PUBLICATIONS DISTRIBUTOR**